BUILDING A CHRISTIAN FAMILY

BUILDING A CHRISTIAN FAMILY

by

KENNETH & ELIZABETH GANGEL

MOODY PRESS

CHICAGO

*We joyfully dedicate this book
to our two "new children"—
our daughter-in-law, Beth, and our son-in-law, Tim—
new members of our family*

Psalm 115:14

© 1987 by
THE MOODY BIBLE INSTITUTE
OF CHICAGO

All Scripture quotations, unless noted otherwise, are from the *Holy Bible: New International Version.* Copyright © 1973, 1978, 1984, International Bible Society. Used by permission of Zondervan Bible Publishers.

Library of Congress Cataloging in Publication Data

Gangel, Kenneth O.
    Building a Christian family.

    Includes bibliographies.
    1. Family—Religious life. I. Gangel, Elizabeth.
II. Title.
BV4526.2.G34   1987   248.4   87-5577
ISBN 0-8024-1506-7

5 6 7 Printing/BC/Year 92 91 90 89

Printed in the United States of America

If you are looking for a comprehensive guide to successful family living, built solidly on traditional biblical values, but geared relevantly to the contemporary scene with its unique problems, the Gangels have provided it for you.

Richard L. Strauss
Pastor
Emmanuel Faith Community Church
Escondido, California

Kenn and Betty Gangel are such dedicated, competent parents and knowledgeable Christian educators that anything they write about the family could be beneficial. *Building a Christian Family* has some unique features that will make it especially helpful. I especially appreciate the sections dealing with children during various phases of their lives. The authors' strong stand on some controversial issues will provoke a lot of good discussion, while their practical suggestions will provide guidance for Christian families in difficult times.

Charles M. Sell
Professor of Christian Education
Trinity Evangelical Divinity School

I have been waiting for a book on the family by Kenneth and Elizabeth Gangel. I have had the privilege of watching this book in the making, not in the usual sense of writing and typing, but in watching the premises lived out in the Gangel home.

Kenn and Elizabeth have a unique ability to apply biblical truth to living circumstances. The largest need of today's families is a foundation—a place to stand. This book ties practical experience to biblical principles in a most convincing manner, and I know it works because I know the Gangel family. You will enjoy this book and be greatly helped by it.

Jay Kesler
President
Taylor University

Contents

Foreword

The family, that safety net for God's people and His purposes, is sometimes viewed in our topsy-turvy world as little more than a cobweb—very sticky, hard to shed, but entirely expendable if one can get free. Song lyrics and love stories chant an ominous theme of unrestraint; young society is free-lancing life. The family is considered a tenacious mesh, and our youth have found an exit door through their fanatical insistence on individual rights, no matter the cost. But an authority higher than the divorce court remains and provides another option: families are, in fact, the only safe deployment for life. Is there still a way to make them work?

Once again, the simple biblical perspective of the family as a protection for growing humans needs a fresh hearing. Kenn and Betty Gangel, having reared two children to thriving adulthood and pastored scores of others in their ministries, combine to tell a new generation what God means by "family." Building a strong family requires liberal interpersonal giving, clear goals, firm direction; the concept of investment is woven throughout. The writers do not take for granted that their readers know even the most traditional principles of parenting. How can a child's behavior be changed from unacceptable to admirable? By what means should he learn about God? Where should he go to school? What kind of recreation does he need? What are the financial considerations? How can he be taught values? Those are daily decisions for dads and moms—choices with lifelong consequences.

Like repainted white lines on the highway, this book redefines the roadway for families at a time when the storm is heavy and steering young lives is a dangerous occupation. As long-time colleagues of the Gangels in the critical pursuit of Christian education, we add our amen to this restatement of eternal truth.

HOWARD AND JEANNE HENDRICKS

Introduction

Discipleship and leadership begin at home. Both Old and New Testament Scriptures indicate that prospective church leaders must have proved records of godliness within their families before they qualify for service in the church. To be sure, there are those who dismiss the recent evangelical emphasis on the family as faddism, but a strong emphasis on the home has been characteristic of believers since the first century.

We are aware that the Waltons no longer live on Walton Mountain. The American family no longer resembles "Family Circle" cartoons or two-parent-two-kid stereotypes. The single adult population may be approaching 60 million, and the number of unmarried men and women living together has topped the 2 million mark.

But what *may* happen is primarily of interest to those who study sociology and anthropology. Biblical Christians concern themselves with what *ought to be,* because they base their lives on God's unchanging Word and unwavering standards. The family may be different, but it's not dead. Sin may stain its potential, but the Savior can salvage its purpose.

To that end we offer this book. It targets young people and adults who are or plan to be partners and parents according to God's plan. Some experts and scholars will fault this effort for its failure to depend heavily on psychological and sociological insights. Although we recognize with appreciation all that those fields of study have done in family life research, our intent is to provide biblical and practical guidelines to help families function as God wants them to. More than 150 biblical texts are cited throughout the chapters, and we urge the reader to consider each one in its scriptural context.

PART ONE

Biblical Foundations

1

What Makes a Home Christian?

The fabric of the family is tearing with an agonizing sound that can be heard throughout the land. Each year more than a million American teenagers become pregnant, four out of five of them unmarried, thirty thousand of them under age fifteen. If the present trends continue, 40 per cent of today's fourteen-year-old girls will be pregnant at least once before the age of twenty.[1]

According to *U.S. News and World Report*, "many Americans today are stretching the boundaries of traditional morality." Research done for the magazine by the Roper Organization and reported in the December 9, 1985, issue indicated that 24 percent of all Americans cheat on their income tax returns, that today's young adults tend to be less honest than their elders in everyday situations, and that 61 percent of those surveyed said it was not wrong for a man and a woman to have sexual relations before marriage.

Meanwhile, Dr. Paul C. Vitz, professor of psychology at New York University, has carried out research on public school textbooks in America. According to Vitz, they are both anti-religious and anti-family.

1. Claudia Wallis, "The Tragic Costs of Teenage Pregnancy," *Readers Digest*, April 1986, p. 99.

The family was often mentioned, but the idea that marriage is the foundation of the family is never presented. The words "marriage," "wedding," "husband," "wife," did not occur once. Nowhere was it suggested that being a mother or homemaker was a worthy and important role for a woman.[2]

No wonder the family is in a state of disintegration in North America. For decades it has been under fire from a variety of powerful enemies. Somehow, however, we want to believe that there ought to be an exception to the statistics—the Christian home. Surely men and women dedicated to Jesus Christ and to each other can stem the tide or, at least, stand as pockets of resistance in a society seemingly hell-bent on destroying the family. Unfortunately, analysis of evangelical churches does not support that notion. Divorce, separation, delinquency, drug use, abortion, unfaithfulness—all the problems that contribute to family breakdown in the society at large seem to have found their way into the Christian community as well.

Yet there are still sterling examples of what God intended when He created marriage and family. Children of God are determined to follow through on the Father's plan and make their homes Christian. What does it take? What makes a home Christian?

BIBLICAL PEOPLE

Christian homes are created by biblical people. We can discern a clear pattern—biblical *people* become biblical *partners*, who can then become biblical *parents*. Only believing people can enter Christian marriage, otherwise the marriage is not Christian. And the process requires us to become partners before we become parents.

Consider Pam,* in her fourth year at a state university. She didn't grow up in a Christian home. In fact, she trusted Christ

---

*Apart from stories about out own family, all family anecdotes and names are fictitious.

2. Paul C. Vitz, "Textbooks Flunk Exam," *Christianity Today,* March 7, 1986, p. 15.

less than a year earlier at a campus Bible study. Now, in her spiritual infancy, she finds herself struggling with her engagement to Larry. Slowly she's beginning to understand the meaning of a Christian home, and, unsure of Larry's spiritual commitment, she finds her heart in turmoil about their future. What are their chances?

What kind of people is God seeking to create and sustain Christian homes in the frenetic final years of this century?

PEOPLE COMMITTED TO THE FAMILY

According to the *Kiplinger Report,* there will be fewer first marriages in the years just ahead. Remarriage will account for a third of all weddings in the late 80s and in the 90s. The number of people never married will double, even though 90 percent of today's young people are expected to get married. In short, fewer people are marrying, and those who do are marrying later.

Such trends need pose no problem for Christians genuinely committed to what God wants in their lives. Doubtless He will call some to singleness, since marriage is not for everyone. Others will decide that God wants them to get married but not have children. The majority, however, will be people committed to the family as a God-given institution and committed, particularly, to their own families.

PEOPLE COMMITTED TO EACH OTHER

One of the most important aspects of the Christian home is an unselfish attitude of loving and giving. Marriage is not like a coat one puts on but, rather, like a flower that grows. Its life depends on the healthy love of each partner for the other and on creative self-giving in which patience, kindness, and gentleness produce growth in both partners. False love tries to find the perfect person and latch on. True love commits itself to another despite the flaws in his or her character.

PEOPLE COMMITTED TO LIFE-LONG LOVE

In Philippians 1:9-10, Paul writes, "That your love may abound more and more in knowledge and depth of insight, so that you may be able to discern what is best and may be pure and blameless until the day of Christ." He speaks of spiritual love to Christ and the church, but the same holds true of marital love between a husband and wife. Popular songs would have us believe that romantic love can be sustained endlessly, but that is a juvenile myth. Love must grow and be protected in a marriage relationship. As Larry Christenson has said, it is not the love that sustains the marriage, but the marriage that sustains the love.

The *Living Bible* (TLB) rendition of 1 Corinthians 13 offers some standards of life-long love, and the following "love test" is based on that passage. How does your love measure up?

Love is a responsiveness to the total self of the one loved.

Love is a feeling of pleasure but also of reverence.

Love is a quality of self-giving.

Love is a willingness to take responsibility as well as to accept joy.

Love is an unusual joy in the company of the other and pain in separation.

Love is a mutual joy and enjoyment of each other without need of physical expression.

Love is a protective attitude evidenced by care for the other person.

Love is a feeling of longing for the loved one.

Love is an inner knowledge that you understand the loved one well.

Love is a growing consistence and maturity and stability.

PEOPLE COMMITTED TO GOD'S WILL

When difficulties come in a marriage relationship (and they always do), we are tempted to retreat into selfishness, to seek and protect our own happiness. But biblical people ask the ultimate question: "What does God want us to do?" The Holy Spirit witnesses inwardly about our salvation, and He can certainly affirm God's will regarding family decisions and marriage relationships. Biblical people don't look first to the sociologists or the psychologists—they look to the Father.

BIBLICAL PURPOSE

Pam sometimes feels that she and Larry have very little in common, and the distance between them seems to be increasing rather than decreasing. It's not because of Larry's personality—he's lots of fun, gentle, attentive, and he even goes to church with Pam every Sunday. But he talks of marriage in his own terms and shows virtually no understanding of God's purposes.

Have you ever wondered why God created marriage in the first place? Has God designed any priorities for the relationship? What does the pastor mean when he says, "Whom God hath joined together, let no man put asunder?" We not only believe God has given us biblical purposes for marriage but that there may even be an order of importance which, if violated, could account for some of the family problems we see all around us today.

COMPLETE COMPANIONSHIP

Companionship stands as the primary purpose of marriage. In spite of all the wonderful things God had created in the Garden of Eden, Adam lived in inadequacy. None of the animals, as splendid as they must have been before the Fall, could provide a fitting companion for the man. At that point the Lord created the first family. Here's how the *Amplified Bible* captures the impact of Genesis 2:18: "Now the Lord God said, It is not good (sufficient, satisfactory) that the man should be alone; I'll make him a helper meet (suitable, adaptable, completing) for him."

The strategic role of fellowship in marriage provides the bull's eye on the family target. Everything else is secondary. Everything else takes a lower place of esteem, because if companionship isn't working, the family isn't working.

SEXUAL FULFILLMENT

The early chapters of Genesis contain no account of the sexual attitudes and activities of Adam and Eve. But throughout the pages of Scripture it seems clear that in Christian marriage, physical sharing flows from spiritual sharing. The mutual responsibilities of husband and wife stare at us from the seventh chapter of 1 Corinthians.

> The husband should fulfill his marital duty to his wife, and likewise the wife to her husband. The wife's body does not belong to her alone but also to her husband. In the same way, the husband's body does not belong to him alone but also to his wife. Do not deprive each other except by mutual consent and for a time, so that you may devote yourselves to prayer. Then come together again so that Satan will not tempt you because of your lack of self-control. (1 Corinthians 7:3-5)

Sexual fulfillment in marriage is a part of God's design and is never to be used as a ploy or tool of manipulation. Such "defrauding" opens our lives to temptation by Satan. Biblical people practicing biblical purposes understand the meaning of Hebrews 13:4: "Marriage should be honored by all, and the marriage bed kept pure, for God will judge the adulterer and all the sexually immoral."

PLANNED PARENTHOOD

How interesting that in a perverted society a good expression like *planned parenthood* should take on negative connotations and get dragged into the horrors of abortion. The crowning glory of children in marriage provides the theme for a song of praise often sung in the pages of Holy Scripture. In two consecutive psalms (127 and 128) we learn that children are a reward from the Lord; they will be "like olive shoots" around the family table. The command to "be fruitful and increase in number and fill the earth" came to both Adam and Noah. God's miracle of procreation continues as a mystery of His grace to expectant parents.

But this purpose cannot be filled by every parent. In some cases God wills parents to be childless, and we must not pass judgment on His will. What seems clear in Scripture is that in most families God designs people to be loving partners and then loving parents.

FAMILY UNITY

Shortly before his death Moses reiterated the law for his nation and emphasized their responsibility as parents (Deuteronomy 6:4-25). The home has always been God's primary place of nurture and growth. In designing marriage the Heavenly Father created a place where children could be nurtured in holy wisdom and faith. God doesn't give children to school systems or church congregations but to families. The very process of reproduction stamps on parents the responsibility to nurture their children through growth and development until they become adults and the cycle begins all over again.

CHURCH SYMBOLISM

Certainly the primary metaphor for the church in the New Testament centers in the human body (Romans 12; 1 Corinthians 12). But in the well-known verses from Ephesians 5, Paul draws a comparison between the husband-wife relationship and Christ and His church. What is the church like? Like a family. How do we understand what the church is supposed to do? We watch godly husbands and wives relating to each other and to their children, and we learn what God intends in the church.

Some Christian families become the only "church" un-saved neighbors ever see. As they watch a husband nourishing and cherishing his family they learn something about the way the Lord nourishes and cherishes the church. As they see a wife respond in submission, and children treat their parents with respect, honoring them with obedience, they learn how God's people respond to the Lord of the church. Your family is a microcosmic demonstration of the Body of Christ in the world.

We recall often a time when our children were very small and we were eating in a restaurant. Another couple, sitting at a nearby table, went unnoticed until they got up to leave and stopped as they walked by our table. They commented about the behavior of our children, calling it a pleasant exception to what they commonly saw in restaurants.

After the initial shock, we took note of the fact that some-one watches and observes the relationships in our family every time we're in public. We were communicating without even being aware of it.

As anyone would, we experienced a slight case of pride that we were such wonderful parents. But God showed us that we were just being His people in the world, demonstrating in living color what the Lord can do in and through His church.

BIBLICAL PRINCIPLES

Marriage is for adults only. As she grows in her Christian life, Pam senses Larry's spiritual indifference. Though he claims to be a believer, his life-style and personal interests rarely support that conclusion. But they have made commitments to each other, and Pam still clings to the hope that things will be different after they are married.

Part of being biblical people ready to embark on a biblical purpose means maintaining a level of maturity ready to handle the different tasks of family relationships and apply biblical principles in those relationships. One could make an endless list of biblical principles for marriage and family living, but let us name just four.

MONOGOMY

What are we to make of Old Testament passages telling us that David and others had multiple wives and yet were greatly loved and blessed of God? Indeed, David is called a man after God's own heart! In looking at the flow of God's truth through both Old and New Testaments we see the initial design as God created it—one man and one woman in the Garden. Then sin entered the world, and all kinds of aberrations became common in human experience. In speaking to the Greeks about idolatry Paul said, "In the past God overlooked such ignorance, but now he commands all people everywhere to repent" (Acts 17:30). As the New Testament opens and the church takes form, it almost seems as though God is starting again with His plan for Christian families. Joseph and Mary offer the purity and beauty of monogamous godly marriage, the spiritual Adam and Eve of the New Covenant. In the midst of the paganism of Graeco-Roman culture, the church stands out as committed to several basic and absolute truths—among them is the purity of marriage relationships.

FIDELITY

What ever happened to "'till death do us part"? In Romans 7 Paul uses that concept as an illustration of the role of the law in Christian living. His illustration reminds us of the finality of the marriage bond: "For example, by law a married woman is bound to her husband as long as he is alive, but if her husband dies, she is released from the law of marriage" (Romans 7:2). Sometimes we talk about marriage being "eternal," but that is not a biblical concept. In heaven there is no marriage (Matthew 22:30)—the termination is a part of God's plan.

HETEROSEXUALITY

Twenty years ago it would not have seemed necessary to emphasize heterosexuality in marriage, but homosexual marriage reflects the perversion of contemporary society. Overwhelming biblical evidence condemns homosexuality. We know of only one episode in history in which God singled out a particular sin and destroyed two entire cities because of it—the sin was homosexuality, and the cities were Sodom and Gomorrah.

Even apart from biblical evidence, homosexuality ought to be condemned by an intelligent culture. Paul Popenoe, founder of the American Institute of Family Relations, once wrote, "Homosexuality . . . is usually found in civilizations that are decaying and approaching disintegration. In no such nation, to my knowledge, has it been promoted so aggressively as in ours in the present time. . . . There is no more reason to allow such persons to continue dragging new victims into their miserable existence, than to allow persons sick with any other serious communicable disease to spread their illness to the public."[3]

For purposes of this book only heterosexual union will be considered "marriage"; we believe that is what the Bible intends to say.

MUTUALITY

Pam feels as though she has been trapped into marrying Larry. He's such an outstanding student and athlete, such a nice guy; her parents have been pressuring her for more than a year not to let him get away. Girl friends have been telling her how lucky she is, so she said yes, and the wedding date has been set. But if Pam marries Larry in response to what other people want for her, there could be big trouble ahead. Mutuality in marriage requires the willingness of each partner to unite two lives and take equal responsibility to make the marriage work. It has been argued that marriage can't be a "fifty-fifty" arrangement, because such a marriage would have no boss. But headship in marriage is another matter. The concept of mutuality means a couple share the responsibility for the outcome and consequences of the marriage.

3. Paul Popenoe, quoted in *The Gospel and the Gay* (Nashville: Thomas Nelson, 1978), pp. 179-80.

Between 1970 and 1984 married couple families fell from 70.5 percent to 58.6 percent, while single parent families are rapidly on the increase.[4] Women currently make up more than 44 percent of the work force, and the age of people marrying continues to climb. But other trends are beginning to emerge. The number of young children in school has been growing as children of the baby boom generation flock to the classroom. By the year 2000 the number of school age children (which dropped to just over 44 million in 1985) is expected to hit 50 million.

How many of those 50 million children will be reared in godly homes? How many will have two parents who love each other, love God, and love them? How many will enjoy the atmosphere of a home as God intended? Only those whose parents genuinely understand what makes a home Christian.

Questions for Discussion

1. Look up all the Scripture references mentioned in this chapter and decide which of them are most important for application to your life and family *now*.
2. Do you think the authors have accurately stated the biblical purposes for marriage? Which are most important to you? Which seem questionable? Why?
3. In what ways are you currently "working at love"? How are you specifically developing a relationship with your husband or wife in order to produce a life-long love?
4. What do you believe about the mutuality of responsibility in Christian marriage? How are you and your mate currently sharing responsibility for family effectiveness?
5. Considering the statistics and trends mentioned in the chapter, what do you see as the major problems facing the Christian family over the next ten years?

4. "Population Profile of the United States," Census Bureau, November 7, 1985.

2

Roles and Relationships in the Christian Home

Trust the *Readers Digest* for homey, real life anecdotes-with-a-point. One that appeared in July of 1986 told the story of a little lost boy in a supermarket. A helpful worker came to his rescue and led him through the aisles looking for his mother. Each time she asked "Do you see your mother?" the boy answered, "No." Finally, she stood him on a counter at the front of the store and asked the question again. This time he replied, "No, I just keep seeing my daddy!"

One could hardly expect the child to answer differently to the question put to him. Obviously, he was not surprised to find his daddy in the supermarket, but the rescue lady never thought to ask the appropriate question. Though deciding which member of the family does the shopping is hardly an example, roles and responsibilities of family members do tend to get confused in today's world. That confusion stands in contrast to the distinct teaching of the Scriptures about what family members are to be and do.

Bishop Moule in his commentary on Colossians quotes a letter from Aristides dated in the immediate post-apostolic era:

Now the Christians, O king, know and believe in God, the maker of heaven and earth, from whom they have received those commandments which they have engraved upon their minds, which they keep, in the hope and expectation of the world to come; so that on his account they do not commit adultery or fornication, they do not bear false witness, they do not deny deposit, or covet what is not theirs; they honor father and mother; their wives are pure as virgins and their daughters modest; and their men abstain from all unlawful wedlock and all impurity in the hope of the recompense that is to come in another world. But as for their servants or hand-maids, or their children, if any of them have any, they persuade them to become Christians, for the love that they have towards them; and when they become so, they call them without distinction, brethren. They walk in all humility and kindness, and falsehood is not found among them; and they love one another.[1]

Roles and relationships in the Christian home are fairly well defined in the Scriptures and haven't changed a great deal despite what some experts may tell us. As we noted in the last chapter, the mutuality of relationship leads to the mutuality of *responsibility,* and that is the key word of this chapter. Each member of the family has his or her own unique function, and that function affects everyone else in the family.

Responsibilities of a Christian Husband/Father

Duane McNeil is about to take on the biggest job of his life. At the age of twenty-eight, he is getting married. Some people would say he is "finally" getting married, but, to Duane, every-thing leading up to his wedding with Tammy fits the careful plan of God. Soon talk must be translated into action and the jokes put behind him. The demands of his accounting career will become secondary to the priorities of his role as a husband

1. H.C.B. Moule, *Colossian Studies* (London: Hodder and Stoughton, 1898), p. 246.

and perhaps one day as a father. From his study of the New Testament, he has determined that his priorities will be to:

LOVE

Love is an action-process verb, not just a passive noun. The word used in the original text in all the passages on the family is *agapao*, the same word used in John 3:16 to describe God's love for the world. Explaining the word in his commentary on the gospel of John, Merrill Tenney writes: "It is the noblest and strongest in Greek. It connotes an act of the will rather than emotion, whim, or infatuation, and its measure is defined in terms of the result."[2] Our perverted society sometimes confuses masculinity with cruelty and harshness, but Scripture indicates that God's first requirement for Christian husbands is that they love their wives. Colossians 3:19 doesn't equivocate: "Husbands, love your wives and do not be harsh with them." That is an unconditional imperative; it is not dependent upon how the wife responds.

The second part of the verse ("do not be harsh") indicates an emphasis on attitude. Biblical husband-love will center not only in feeling but in fact; not only in emotion, but in devotion; not only in attitude, but in action. Proverbs 31 contains a portrait of the ideal woman. Might there have been an ideal man behind the scenes of that beautiful chapter? If so, he was a husband who allowed freedom for his wife, affirming her identity and purpose, and appreciating what she meant to the family and the home.

LEAD

In one of his counseling sessions, Duane's pastor asked him if he could quote any verses from 1 Corinthians 11. He started on some of the "body" verses from chapter 12 and some thoughts on love from chapter 13 but couldn't remember any of

2. Merrill Tenney, *John—the Gospel of Belief* (Grand Rapids: Eerdmans, 1948), p. 89.

chapter 11. The pastor went on to explain that the husband's leadership forms the core of the Christian home: "Now I want you to realize that the head of every man is Christ, and the head of the woman is man, and the head of Christ is God" (v. 3). To be sure, this passage swims in controversy, and some have argued that "headship" is something other than leadership responsibility, but the historic (and we think correct) understanding of the term is that it refers to the authority of the husband.

Fathers who desert their families create the major source of poverty in the United States. Some fathers create a major source of spiritual poverty in the homes in which they live. Duane has never led a family before, but he understands that headship and submission as designed by God provide a husband and wife with the ideal way of relating to one another, and he intends to learn to do it God's way.

LABOR

Paul wrote to the young Christian leader Timothy, "If anyone does not provide for his relatives, and especially for his immediate family, he has denied the faith and is worse than an unbeliever" (1 Timothy 5:8). The husband serves as provider and protector for his wife and as father for his children. Perhaps if more husbands provided more adequately, fewer wives would have to work and leave their children in day care centers or with relatives. There are exceptions, of course, that may temporarily prevent husbands from fulfilling their roles as providers: illness, times of unemployment, and periods of schooling. But the general principle of caring for one's wife and children has never changed since the days of Timothy.

LEARN

Duane will have to *learn* to love, *learn* to lead, and *learn* to labor for his family. But he also has to *learn* so that he can teach. First Corinthians 14:35 tells wives to ask their husbands at home any questions that might come into their minds at church. In his personal Bible study, Duane has found passages such as Deuteronomy 6 and Ephesians 6, which emphasize a husband's responsibility to teach his wife and a father's responsibility to teach his children. He is determined that Tammy will be able to ask him questions about the Bible and Christian living and receive intelligent, spiritual answers. He is determined that they will be able to study and pray together, not only in a time of worship, but as a way of fulfilling the responsibilities God has set before them.

RESPONSIBILITIES OF A CHRISTIAN WIFE/MOTHER

Tammy has begun preparation for marriage as well, and she and Duane have spent time discussing their plans. At first some of the things he said seemed old-fashioned and out of touch with what she had heard at college. But as they studied Scripture together she began to see the bigger picture and understand *her* scriptural responsibilities as well. For example, she sees that she needs to:

SUBMIT

God tells wives to be constantly subjecting themselves in obedience to their own husbands. The word is *hupotasso*, so frequently used in the second and third chapters of 1 Peter. It is a military term that means to place in proper rank. God arranged the family in an orderly way so that someone would shoulder the responsibility for headship and someone would accept the responsibility of followership.

How unfortunate that some have distorted this frequently stated command of Scripture into a chauvinistic attack against equality. The major error comes in misunderstanding what Paul says in both Colossians and Ephesians. God's command of submission in no way implies inferiority of wives or women. The passages don't deal with essence or equality at all, but with *function.*

An understanding of the doctrine of the Trinity can help us here. Jesus Christ is equal with the Father; They are both God. Yet during the days of His earthly ministry the Lord frequently spoke of doing only those things that the Father had commanded and being constantly sensitive to the Father's will. The godly wife submits voluntarily and joyfully because she knows it is part of her biblical responsibility.

SUPPORT

We spoke earlier of the ideal wife described in Proverbs 31. This woman formed the backbone of her family. She encouraged her husband and solidified her family. In this particular case, perhaps she even supported them financially to some degree, but that is not the main focus. To be supportive as a wife is to be encouraging and sustaining, someone who holds things together. Tammy finds something in her personality that genuinely warms to that kind of commitment. She expects to be able to fulfill it quite comfortably.

STABILIZE

As we look at the great women of the Bible we see that they provided a stable balancing point for their families. Sarah, Rebecca, Hannah, Mary, Priscilla—each one fulfilled the description of Proverbs 31. Perhaps Peter had some of them in mind when he referred to the inner beauty of godly wives as beauty

> of your inner self, the unfading beauty of a gentle and quiet spirit, which is of great worth in God's sight. For this is the way the holy women of the past who put their hope in God used to make themselves beautiful. They were submissive to their own husbands, like Sarah, who obeyed Abraham and called him her master. You are her daughters if you do what is right and do not give way to fear. (1 Peter 3:4-6)

Such are the qualities of a biblical wife.

SOCIALIZE

She's struggling with it, but Tammy has determined not to let *homemaker* be a negative term in her thinking. At the age of twenty-five she's grappling with Paul's wise words to Titus: "Likewise, teach the older women to . . . train the younger women to love their husbands and children, to be self-controlled and pure, to be busy at home, to be kind, and to be subject to their husbands, so that no one will malign the Word of God" (Titus 2:3-5). She understands that while Duane works at his office day after day, the task of making family decisions and running the home will be up to her. Tammy wants to think of that not as drudgery, or even just domestic duty, but as genuine service for Jesus Christ. Making a home a place of spiritual sociability will be largely her responsibility, and she looks forward to it.

RESPONSIBILITIES OF CHRISTIAN CHILDREN

Will Duane and Tammy have children? It's too early to tell, but they certainly hope so. And when they do, they want those children to be as much a part of the family unit as Mom and Dad. All family members will share family responsibilities. For the kids, that will mean they are to:

OBEY

The marvelous passage in Colossians 3 we referred to earlier also deals with relationships between parents and children. The first word of verse 21 *(pateras)* can properly be translated "parents" rather than "fathers." Perhaps in this context, that is the preferred translation (see Hebrews 11:23).

The apostle synthesizes New Testament teaching to Christian children in the home by focusing on the main command —obedience. The word translated "children" in verse 20 is the word *teknon*, which points to birth and offspring relationship, not to age. In our society we stop using the word *child* when youngsters become teenagers, but the Greeks used *teknon* to identify family relationships well beyond the adolescent years. According to biblical standards, teenagers stand under the rubric of obedience. The word for "obey," used in Acts 12:13 to describe responding to a knock at the door, came to mean paying attention to any command.

The word "everything" is interesting, isn't it? Do your children obey in *everything*? Do you know any children who obey in *everything*? Yet Bishop Lightfoot, in commenting on this passage, indicates that "the rule is stated absolutely, because the exceptions are so few that they may be disregarded."[3]

Parents, of course, have a major responsibility here, as verse 21 emphasizes: "Do not embitter your children or they will become discouraged." Phillips translates this verse, "Parents, don't overcorrect your children." Puritan austerity, with its focus on silence and the blind following of every verbal command, perverts biblical patterns as much as the overpermissiveness and rebellion that tend to characterize our society today. The Bible is clear—*children obey.*

HONOR

Ephesians 6 begins by telling children first to obey and then, immediately following, to "honor your father and mother —which is the first commandment with a promise—that it may go well with you and that you may enjoy long life on the earth." Paul refers to Deuteronomy 5:16. He points up that God wants more than just blind or even reluctant obedience from children in a Christian home; He wants them to obey in a way that honors, respects, and demonstrates the right attitude toward their parents. Christian obedience functions in a new dimension, far different from a private's response to a nasty drill sergeant at boot camp.

3. J.B. Lightfoot, *Saint Paul's Epistles to the Colossians and to Philemon* (London: MacMillan, 1879), p. 227.

REPAY

Paul writes something peculiar to Timothy. He says widows' children or grandchildren "should learn first of all to put their religion into practice by caring for their own family and so repaying their parents and grandparents, for this is pleasing to God" (1 Timothy 5:4). The one word rendered "repaying" in the English text is actually two words in the Greek text and can literally be translated "to return returns." It carries the double impact of both verb and noun to emphasize a third biblical duty of children.

Most of us would be happy for our children to repay us by making good use of their opportunities, rearing their own families for the Lord, and continuing to love Christ and His church throughout their lives. Parents and grandparents would consider themselves well "repaid" to see that kind of return on their investment.

But this verse speaks not about spiritual response; it deals with financial and economic concerns. In short, children are responsible to take care of their parents and grandparents when the latter reach an age at which care may be necessary. We have become so accustomed to the welfare state, Medicare, Medicaid, pensions, and retirement programs that we forget the initial responsibility of caring for aging parents does not rest with the government but with their children. Christian children sensitive to Scripture understand that they have a responsibility to repay when and as their parents need their help.

A marvelous mutuality pervades all these relationships; they are the ongoing responsibility of both parties or, in some cases, all parties. If we accept biblical norms for behavior in our Christian homes, people will be happier, partners will be happier, parents will be happier, children will be happier, and the church will feel the impact, since local congregations are simply families of families. When each family member performs his God-given responsibilities, the Christian family can provide our society with a beam of light in the darkness, a tiny grain of salt in the rotting pottage of our corrupting culture.

Questions for Discussion

1. Do you believe the authors' description of biblical roles are accurate? If not, in what ways would you change them?
2. Do the scriptural passages on family responsibilities apply with full force in today's world?
3. What additional responsibilities might you find for a Christian husband? Father?
4. What additional responsibilities might you add for a Christian wife? Mother?
5. What additional responsibilities might you add for Christian children? Siblings?

3

Godly Standards in the Modern Home

Sandy and her friend Kim have just hit fifteen. Last week they went to their first "real" party, a get-together of about twenty kids after a basketball game. There was no parental supervision; they were allowed to go with their dates, who were two or three years older than they. And though both girls are Christians, most of the kids at the party were not.

The loud rock music and dancing offered no surprise, and they expected heavy beer drinking, even by members of the team. But late in the evening something happened that changed their lives. Their dates took them to a bedroom at the back of the house and invited them to share a joint of marijuana. As the cigarette was passed around the small group gathered there, they said no, stuck with it, and paid the price in teasing for the rest of the party. But that evening proved a significant milestone in their spiritual growth—they each made a personal, independent decision regarding right and wrong.

Why would they make a choice like that? Why would there even be a problem? On the other hand, what kind of family backgrounds provided them with the resources to make the choice most Christians would consider right? Christian parents and evangelical churches struggle to identify and teach absolute standards of biblical morality and ethics without superimposing their own particular interpretations or peculiarities on what the Bible says, but morality is often a moving target. The key word is *absolute* (a principle or truth that does not change), and our society has virtually thrown over absolutes, particularly in the realm of morality and ethics.

On certain subjects, Americans have simply changed their minds. Gambling used to be widely condemned. Now churches run Bingo games, and twenty-two states and the District of Columbia operate lotteries. At one time, consumption of alcohol was widely condemned. Now nearly two-thirds of Americans drink at least occasionally.[1]

This chapter is designed to help parents teach their children and teenagers to live godly lives in a culture designed to make them ungodly.

CONFLICTS IN THE BATTLE FOR STANDARDS

We agree with Paul Vitz, who said, "A Christian theory of moral education must start with the assumption of God's revelation of the moral life to mankind as expressed in Scripture and understood in Church. The moral understanding of the human condition revealed in Scripture clearly acknowledges man's capacity for evil . . . [and] it provides a clear basis for knowing what should be done."[2] To understand the battle, we must understand the conflicts.

BETWEEN PRODUCT AND PROCESS

Christians can agree to some extent on the kind of product they would like to see come out of their homes after eighteen years, but they may vastly disagree on the process required to produce the product. Proverbs 22:6 is abused when parents take it as an ironclad promise rather than a guideline. Perhaps

1. "Morality," *U.S. News and World Report,* December 9, 1985, p. 55.
2. Paul C. Vitz, "Toward a Christian Model of Moral Development," *New Oxford Review,* September 1981, p. 20.

the best translation of the phrase "in the way he should go" would be "according to his own individual, unique way." The process requires personalization, individualization, and a willingness to recognize that the rules of child rearing change with each child who enters the home.

BETWEEN OBJECTIVES

Should Christian young people be allowed to dance or not? Should they listen to rock music or not? Is social drinking in the Christian home harmless or harmful? Christians don't agree on the answers to these questions. We need to understand that, regardless of the position we take as parents, our children will be playing and talking with youngsters from families with widely varying sets of standards. Strict legal codes of what we "do" and "don't do" are not particularly helpful. Our kids need to develop convictions and standards linked to the teaching of God's Word.

BETWEEN PARENTAL AND YOUTH VALUES

How democratic can a family be? We used the old family council system for years and found it quite helpful, but there were always certain things that the parents alone had the right to determine. The kids can take the role of Congress and send a bill to the White House, but Christian parents cannot abdicate God-given authority in some basic decisions that affect the family.

But God-given authority exercised lovingly in a participatory setting cannot be equated with playing absolute monarch over the lives of all family members. When we talk out various problems and issues discussing the biblical principles behind our decisions and guidelines, children begin to grasp the idea that Mom and Dad are not being capricious or whimsical in setting the house rules. Though they will not always agree with your decisions, your children should be able to give you credit for trying to maintain fairness.

Let's take another look at Kim. Already under a pile of classes, yearbook responsibilities, drama club, and dates, she comes home and announces she wants to try out for cheerleading. Should her parents agree? Should they "protect her from herself" by not letting her get involved in too many activities?

Morality and ethics are not really involved in such a question, so it becomes a matter of what is best for Kim at this time in her life. Wise parents will steer toward a mutual decision, one that takes into consideration such things as her grades, the kind of time commitment that she would have to invest in cheerleading, and what family sacrifices might be necessary if she were chosen for the cheerleading squad. One of the key factors will be to determine how well Kim is handling the commitments she already has.

Giving Kim some of the responsibility for decision-making will increase her self-respect, her commitment to the family, and will probably enhance the value of the collective decision.

BETWEEN INTERPRETATIONS

Sometimes what we call "teaching biblical principles" is nothing more than forcing our own interpretation of Scripture upon our children to the point that their "godly living" becomes an enactment of hand-me-down rules.

Remember Abraham's lie about his relationship to Sarah, used to get himself out of trouble (Genesis 12:13)? He uses it not once, but twice (Genesis 20:1-2). What happens? Isaac catches on to the trick and in a similar situation uses the same lie about Rebecca. When it's Jacob's turn, he can't be bothered with petty half truths and deceptions. He walks into his father's bedroom and says to Isaac, now totally blind, "I am Esau, your first born" (Genesis 27:19). Children tend to imitate their parents in both the good and the bad. Make sure your children learn discernment in interpreting Scripture for themselves under the guidance of the Holy Spirit.

BETWEEN LEGALISM AND LICENSE

Remember Paul's great words to the Galatians? Check Galatians 3:1-5 and 5:1. The Galatians had no problem accepting God's grace for salvation, but then they wanted to write a whole code of Christian conduct based largely on Mosaic teachings. Paul tried to point out that living for Christ *after* salvation is just as much an act of faith and grace as the salvation itself.

The opposite of legalism is license, and Peter addresses that problem very clearly: "Live as free men, but do not use your freedom as a cover-up for evil; live as servants of God" (1 Peter 2:16). The joyful biblical balance between legalism and license is *liberty*, which comes when one lives his life in accordance with the principles (standards) of God's Word.

CONVICTIONS IN THE BATTLE FOR STANDARDS

The development of Christian convictions is a process, not an event.[3] Like their adult mentors, Christian children and young people need to "grow in grace and in the knowledge of our Lord and Savior, Jesus Christ." Many crises in the Christian life require experience for wise decison making, but the development of godly standards is a proved step toward crisis prevention. Among others, you will want to discuss with your child the following convictions.

BODY CONTROL

Many of the temptations we face are body-related—drugs, alcohol, obesity, anorexia, bulemia, illicit sex in various forms—surely God has given some instruction regarding the use of our bodies. It would be helpful to read 1 Corinthians 6:13-20. Here are the last two verses of that passage as they appear in *The Living Bible*.

---

3. This section adapted from Kenneth O. Gangel, *The Family First* (Winona Lake, Ind.: BMH, 1979), pp. 92-98.

Haven't you yet learned that your body is the home of the Holy Spirit God gave you, and that He lives within you? Your own body does not belong to you. For God has bought you with a great price. So use every part of your body to give glory back to God, because He owns it.

That's pretty clear, isn't it? Properly applied, this biblical standard could eliminate many controversial questions about behavior. Coming to grips with the indwelling Christ affords a major step on the road to sanctification. Every Christian of any age has to realize, "God lives in me; where I go, God goes; what I eat, God eats; what I read, God reads." The contextual emphasis deals with immorality, but general application aims at Spirit control of one's entire body at all times.

SELF-EDIFICATION

Paul writes about freedom in 1 Corinthians 10:23, "'Everything is permissible'—but not everything is beneficial. 'Everything is permissible'—but not everything is constructive." This standard states that Christians ought to be doing things, thinking things, going to places, and acting in ways that will build up their lives and make them more like Jesus. Standing on guard against things that can harm us is only half the battle. Paul urges us to go one step further and ask, "How does this help me as a Christian?"

HABIT FREEDOM

At the beginning of the passage on sexual immorality in 1 Corinthians 6, Paul writes, "Everything is permissible for me —but I will not be mastered by anything." So freedom from habits is not a question of rules but of responsibility. Christian living can't be legislated, but it can be learned. Does alcohol master people? Yes. Do drugs master those who take them? Yes. What about homosexuality? Anger? Bitterness? Envy? Depression? Answer the questions yourself, and consider the importance of communicating principles of habit freedom to children and teenagers in the Christian home.

LIFE TESTIMONY

The entire eighth chapter of 1 Corinthians forms the argument aiming toward the final and key verse (v. 13): "Therefore, if what I eat causes my brother to fall into sin I will never eat meat again so that I will not cause him to fall." Should Christians who might believe that beverage alcohol is perfectly acceptable be careful when and how or even if they drink? What about the television shows we watch when guests are in our homes? What kind of language or even attitudes do we display around our children? The standard is clear—I *am* my brother's keeper to the extent that I am responsible if my behavior causes him to fall into sin. That's a tough standard in a society constantly looking out for number one.

When Sandy reflects back to the party after the basketball game, she whispers a prayer of thanks to God for giving her the courage to live up to her convictions. Opportunities to share her faith and explain why she does or does not behave certain ways have dramatically increased since that night. What she first thought might bring ostracism from the group, God turned into credibility among her friends. Sandy has developed a reputation as a "genuine" Christian.

CHRIST PREEMINENT

The last principle seems all comprehensive in that the first four lead to it and are contained in it. As presented in Colossians 1:18, it involves a recognition of the Lord-disciple relationship so essential to Christian living. In describing the supremacy of Christ, Paul writes, "He is the head of the body, the church; he is the beginning and the firstborn from among the dead, so that in everything he might have the supremacy." The growing Christian shouldn't fuss about his own rights, civil or otherwise. Crucified disciples practice the brief but poignant life philosophy of John the Baptist: "He must become greater; I must become less" (John 3:30).

COMMITMENTS IN THE BATTLE FOR STANDARDS

Developing godly life-styles in ourselves and our children presents an ongoing struggle. No wonder Isaac Watts wrote with tongue-in-cheek, "Is this vile world a friend to grace, to help us on to God?" Of course not! Let's never commit that error of judgment. What kinds of commitment are required in this battle? How should a parent begin?

START EARLY

When should a parent start teaching standards? As early as possible. Certainly by the time the preschool child can carry on an intelligent conversation about right and wrong. The development of Christian standards should begin with very young children; they can rarely be superimposed upon college students. Remember Timothy? Paul may have taught him how to preach and hand out tracts, but Grandma and Mom taught him God's truth from the Old Testament long before the apostle ever visited his town (2 Timothy 1:3-7). Those little life-building experiences provide the glue by which godly standards hang together.

But before Mom and Dad begin, they must have their own values, ethics, and standards of morality sorted out. Ignore those who claim that parents shouldn't superimpose their ideas upon their children. That is precisely what the Bible commands us to do! Let's just be sure we have developed those standards through the leading of the Holy Spirit in open-minded understanding of God's Word.

BE PATIENT

Patience is required for the process of moving children from dependence to independence. We've spent almost thirty years working with college and seminary students, and some things about their behavior stand out. Some, particularly college freshmen, come to school unable to handle even the smallest decision because they were refused the opportunity of questioning and reasoning and were forced into a position of *dependence too long.*

The opposite problem surfaces when parents offer *independence too soon.* Students given too much liberty are marked by a general attitude of rebellion and a growing distaste for authority. The solution? Patience, and the ability to spread the process from birth to adulthood.

STICK WITH IT

Think of that great verse in Hebrews: "Therefore, strengthen your feeble arms and weak knees. Make level paths for your feet, so that the lame may not be disabled but rather healed" (Hebrews 12:12-13). It almost seems alien to the context, but, remember, it follows a major section on God's discipline of His children and also the discipline by earthly fathers of their children. I think the writer tells us plainly that such things don't come easily. Too many parents make a good start but never finish because they simply can't stick with it.

TRUST GOD

We're talking here about a life change. Certainly parents can imprint their children, conditioning them to behave in certain ways. That has the potential for both positive and negative outcomes. But in the final analysis, the standards that last on into adult years are rooted in belief systems planted in the hearts of our children by the Heavenly Father Himself. Godly parents, using the power of the Holy Spirit and the dynamic of the Bible, bathing the entire process in prayer, can win the battle.

When our own children were young, we dogmatically made decisions for them—carefully selecting television programs, providing close supervision when they played with certain neighborhood friends; we regulated their bedtimes, what they ate, and when they went to church. We did not consider such issues open for discussion.

During their preteen and teenage years however, we engaged in a great deal of dialogue with our children. They were actively involved in the decision-making process. Their opinions were encouraged and valued. However, final authority still rested with us as their parents.

Now with both of our children married and establishing their own Christian homes, it is a joy to watch as they make decisions based on the principles of God's Word. The root was planted many years ago, and the plants watered regularly. Now it's our turn to watch the fruit grow and ripen.

Yet all across the world there are godly parents with broken hearts because their children, now young adults, have apparently departed from everything they were taught in earlier years. Tom and Ruth Holt have three children now in their late twenties or early thirties. Their oldest daughter, Jan, serves as a missionary in Hong Kong, where she lives with her husband and two children. Tom, Jr., and his family live near his parents and are active in their church. But the day young Mary Holt walked out of her home to go to college marked the beginning of an era of rebellion and bitterness that continues to the present. She has verbally denounced the faith of her parents and apparently turned her back on all Christian values.

How sternly does God hold parents responsible for that kind of apparent apostasy? Without contradicting the enormous responsibility we have for our children while they live in our homes (see the first four chapters of 1 Samuel), there is an interesting balance-wheel passage in the eighteenth chapter of Ezekiel. The prophet quotes an ancient proverb, "The fathers eat sour grapes, and the children's teeth are set on edge," and then relates Jehovah's message: "You will no longer quote this proverb in Israel" (vv. 2-3).

What follows is a specific and detailed outline of the relationship between a responsible adult and God. The Bible seems to teach that God holds parents responsible for their children's behavior during childhood and teen years but gives young adults the option to do precisely what they wish. At that point the Lord holds the new adult responsible, assuming the parents have done their part in raising him for Christ while they had influence over him in the home.

The key paragraph begins at verse 19:

> Yet you ask, "Why does the son not share the guilt of his father?" Since the son has done what is just and right and has been careful to keep all my decrees, he will surely live. The soul who sins is the one who will die. The son will not share the guilt of the father, nor will the father share the guilt of the son. The righteousness of the righteous man will be credited to him, and the wickedness of the wicked will be charged against him. (Ezekiel 18:19-20)

Let's take seriously the business of developing internalized standards so that when our children come to adulthood they will voluntarily choose the righteous path God places before them. But if they choose otherwise, and if we have been faithful in bringing them through the process of developing godly standards, remember that God has absolved us of guilt in their behavior. They must answer before the Lord.

Questions for Discussion

1. The authors raise two unanswered questions (pp. 34 and 40). How would you respond to them?
2. As a parent, how have you experienced some of the conflicts described? For example, how would you assess the difference between your values and those of your children?
3. In what specific ways can Christian parents provide their children with liberty while avoiding both legalism and license?
4. Which of the life-style problems your family is facing could be solved or at least helped by practicing the convictions listed?

5. For what reasons might parents be reluctant to start the process of developing godly standards? What kinds of things tend to get in the way of finishing the job?

PART TWO

Age Group Guidelines

4

Preparing to Be Parents

For whatever reason, people in our day marry and have their children later in life. We've called attention to the trends and statistics earlier, but the fact bears repeating here, because, in one sense at least, it is a positive trend. In the past people in our society tended to marry in their early twenties or maybe even late teens. Preparation for marriage was almost nonexistent, and, in the absence of effective contraceptive devices, preparation for children fared little better. It may very well be that young adults who wait until their mid or late twenties to marry, and then invest time in getting to know each other before children enter the home, have a better crack at effective parenting.

Jack and Jean Whitney are expecting their first baby. Eagerly waiting and planning for his arrival, Jean has been fixing up the nursery, while Jack has been buying little toys. But the truth is that neither one of them is ready for the adjustments that will be necessary when the baby arrives.

When the day comes and the long wait is over, the doctor proudly announces the arrival of a healthy baby boy. After a few days Jack takes Jean and the baby home—and then the problems start.

Their life as parents is simply not what they expected. The baby takes a lot of Jean's time. He cries all night and sleeps all day. Jack thinks he's being neglected, and Jean feels like a prisoner in her own home. Their uneasiness creates an atmosphere of tension rather than the loving climate the baby needs during his first crucial months.

A baby learns love, trust, and security from the firm but gentle hands and arms that hold him and minister to his needs hour by hour. Jack and Jean need to find a way to satisfy baby's physical needs without allowing the entire family's schedule to revolve around him.

UNDERSTANDING BIBLICAL CONCEPTS OF PARENTING

A great deal of marriage counseling deals with relationships between the husband and wife, and well it should. But once those *partner* relationships have been built, *parental* relationships rise to a new priority. What do parents need to know?

THE TRUE NATURE OF CHILDREN

Parents need to understand not only the nature of their own children, but the true nature of all children born into the human race. Viewing children as essentially good leads to a permissive family government. For too long we have been led to believe that children left to their own devices and given ample love will develop in positive directions.

The Bible teaches that children are neither good nor neutral at birth (Psalm 51:5; Ephesians 2:3). They possess a sin nature that must be controlled and ultimately changed by the power of God. In understanding that, the wise parent exercises a benevolent authority given by God.

HOW TO CARE

The Heavenly Father is the perfect model here (1 Peter 5:7). Whatever happens in our lives, however far we might stray, however rebellious we might become, the Father cares for us. Myron R. Chartier puts it well when he writes, "As parents become caring persons to their children, they point beyond themselves to a greater reality: an eternal God who cares."[1]

HOW TO GIVE

How much has the Heavenly Father given us? One need only review John 3:16 and similar passages to see the generosity demonstrated in God's sacrificial love. To be sure, some parents may give too much of themselves or attempt to substitute material gifts for personal love and intimacy. Biblical family sacrifice follows the model of the Heavenly Father with the children following the example of their parents. The result? Mutual family giving.

HOW TO RESPECT THEIR CHILDREN

Small wonder the writer of the book of Hebrews recalls the dramatic language of Psalm 8, "What is man that you are mindful of him, the son of man that you care for him? You made him a little lower than the angels; you crowned him with glory and honor and put everything under his feet" (Hebrews 2:6b-8a). We are the children of the Father and the brothers of Jesus, created in the image of God. How does that translate into a daddy's behavior toward his children? Again we are indebted to Chartier for useful insights:

> If parents are to follow the pattern of God in Jesus Christ, their methods of parenting need to conform to the way of the cross. Each child is created in the dignity of God's image and has the right to become his or her own unique person. Whatever disciplinary measures we use with children must account for this dimension of respect. It is important to interpret to children the consequences of the choices they make, but it is extremely important that they have the right to

1. Myron R. Chartier, "A Theology of Parenting: An Incarnational Model," *American Baptist Quarterly*, March 1984, p. 77.

choose. Children themselves will become respecting persons
to the degree that they have experienced respect.[2]

HOW TO FORGIVE THEIR CHILDREN

Two thousand years ago our Lord taught His disciples to
pray, "Forgive us our sins for we also forgive everyone who sins
against us" (Luke 11:4). That theme is reiterated throughout the
New Testament (Colossians 3:13). A song says, "You always
hurt the one you love, the one you shouldn't hurt at all." That's
certainly true in the family. Perhaps because the family offers
the greatest opportunity for hurt, it also offers the greatest opportunity for forgiveness, but not as a substitute for either discipline or punishment. All three coexist within the framework of a
healthy home when parents both punish effectively and forgive
completely.

Answering Key Questions About Parenting

As we have already seen with some frequency, marriage
forces us to constant and important relationships. Words such
as *compatibility, mutuality, affection,* and *partnership* testify to
the people-contact ratio of marriage and family living. Many of
the crucial questions that haunt the marriage relationship surface between the wedding and the birth of the first child. Consider some of them.

WHY DID WE GET MARRIED?

When Christian couples raise the question of why they
married, the clamoring voices of a secular society provide confusion rather than clarity. Some suggest that the family no longer serves as a primary social group in Western culture. Others
tell us that experimental living together offers a wise way to
enter marriage. Certainly permanency is not considered essential in our society. (Perhaps at this point it would be a good
idea to review again the emphasis of chapter 1, particularly our

2. Chartier, p. 81.

study of the purpose of marriage.) Cultivating mature love is a full-time and lifetime job. A wedding provides the beginning, and the immature quality of love experienced at that moment must be stabilized and nurtured through the years ahead.

HOW MANY CHILDREN SHOULD WE HAVE?

Each couple must determine individually the number of children they will have. Society has its arguments about population control, and Grandma and Grandpa may be clamoring for more grandchildren. The wise Christian husband and wife, however, ask the Lord and each other some pointed questions: Why do we want to have children? How many children will be best for us? How is the Holy Spirit leading us in this matter? When do we want our first child? How soon will we really be ready to be parents?

Hours of open discussion and joint prayer can provide spiritual and intelligent answers to these important questions. God will show us His will.

WHO WILL BE RESPONSIBLE FOR THE BABY?

Parents are ultimately responsible for the children they bring into the world. But with an ever increasing percentage of mothers in the work force, many Christian parents are only too eager to place the new baby with a sitter or in a nursery school as soon as possible so Mom can get back to her job. We believe that is a mistake unless it is absolutely necessary to sustain economic survival in the family. Dramatic personality changes occur during the first few years of childhood, and the child's environment inserts a significant ingredient. Christian parents need to do all they can to make their home a place in which children will learn and grow while feeling secure and loved.

HOW CAN WE SHARE THE RESPONSIBILITIES?

Let's take a closer look at Jean and Jack and their new baby to see how the situation can be changed to develop a healthy and happy atmosphere. Because Jean will be with the baby more hours than Jack, she has a greater responsibility to be sure the baby is fed, bathed, changed, well, and happy. When those essentials are cared for, she need not jump and run each time the baby cries. If she does, he'll soon learn to cry in order to bring someone rushing in to play with him or hold him.

Jean could also make an effort to keep the baby awake during the late afternoon and early evening so that Jack will have time to spend with him, and maybe he'll be ready to sleep at bedtime. Then Jack and Jean can have some time together without being constantly interrupted by the care of the baby.

But Jack has an important role too. He can encourage and support Jean by taking the baby for a while when he gets home from work, perhaps while she's preparing dinner. In addition, Jack's spiritual responsibility has taken on new dimensions, because now he has a son to teach and train in the things of the Lord. Parental dedication can't wait until the baby is six or seven years old.

HOW IMPORTANT IS THE FAMILY SETTING?

Children receive the all-important lifeblood of security and love from their families. There they begin to understand God's pattern of behavior and the development of Christian character, which God has instructed us to carry out (Deuteronomy 6:4-8). The first year is not too early to begin teaching obedience. After a child has been put to bed for the night he needs to learn to stay there. Displeasure and firmness of parental authority can be demonstrated even before full explanation is possible. Where did we get the idea that everybody else in the family must give in to the baby in order to keep peace?

Baby needs to learn respect for other children's toys and for trinkets and flowers so dear to his parents' hearts. The family forms a school in which the small child's relationship to others develops and matures as his parents guide, teach, show kindness, and develop obedience.

ENTERING INTO THE DISCIPLINE OF PARENTING

Isn't it interesting that when we use the word *discipline* we are almost always thinking about what parents do to and for their children? Even before partners become parents they need to give attention to what could very well be called the discipline or discipleship of parenting.

RELATE PROPERLY TO EACH OTHER

Talking about love and harmony is a step toward happiness, but we can never expect talk to become reality until we commit ourselves to the biblical roles discussed in chapter 2. This might be a good place to review Colossians 3:18-21. Remember that children respond as much to their parents' love for each other as to their parents' love for them.

None of the commands of the Colossians passage seem popular in our day. Evangelical feminists criticize biblical subjection, recreational sex has diluted marital love and ruined fidelity, and the permissive society has made obedience to parents an anachronism of pre-World War II America.

Be careful of motives here. Some parents want children for selfish motives—to complete their own lives, to hold their marriages together, to take care of them in their old age, or to provide companionship while the other partner is away. Our churches, our nation, and our world desperately need children who have been loved, disciplined, and nurtured by parents who see *their* children as *God's* children and equate parenting with stewardship. Such parents bring glory to God through child-rearing.

EVERY CHILD IS DIFFERENT

As the years pass, Jack and Jean begin to feel more comfortable about their role as parents. Then a new baby arrives —another boy. Within weeks they discover that each child has his own distinct personality and must be handled individually. Little Nathan is less demanding, constantly content, and even a little shy. His parents love him deeply, sense the difference of personality and needs from those of his older brother, but face the temptation of neglecting their younger son simply because he seems to demand less attention and fewer expressions of love.

Even a casual understanding of the gospels reminds us of the individual and different ways Jesus treated the Twelve—His spiritual children. Every parent who has had more than one child knows that no two are alike and that they cannot be dealt with in the same way.

But some basic guidelines apply to every child. Just because the second one may be strong-willed and difficult to handle, we dare not give in just to avoid conflict. On the other hand if one of the children is shy and sensitive, we don't withhold necessary punishment just because of his or her retiring personality. When God says, "If you refuse to discipline your son, it proves you don't love him" (Proverbs 13:24, TLB), He is talking about all children. Our approach to respect, discipling, punishment, and nurture may be different from child to child, but they must be set in place for *all* the children.

CREATE A SPIRITUAL ATMOSPHERE

We intend to say it often throughout the pages of this book—a proper family atmosphere is the key to effective Christian nurture in the home. Paul Meier uses the term *devotional atmosphere* and describes it as "loving, communicating, planning with your children, exhibiting the fruits of the Spirit and having some good sacred music on from time to time geared to the ages of your children."[3]

STICK TO THE BASICS

Children learn essentially through three things that happen (or should happen) in their homes. The most commonly talked

3. Paul D. Meier, *Christian Child-Rearing and Personality Development* (Grand Rapids: Baker, 1977), p. 153.

about and yet the least important is *instruction*. Instruction is important all right, but it just doesn't measure up to the other two as learning opportunities for young children. The middle item in our triad is *modeling*, and importance of parental example could never be overemphasized when we talk about the discipleship process. Children learn through imitation and, in that sense, any parent who is home becomes a model—good or bad—whether he likes it or not. But the most important aspect of discipleship is *experience*. Every time something happens in the home (pricked fingers, injured pets, special holidays, deaths, births, and so on) a teachable moment appears. The wise, godly parent will immediately use that event or experience as an opportunity to communicate biblical values. That's discipleship.

DEVELOP CHRISTIAN ATTITUDES

Educators call this the *affective* dimension of learning. Parents constantly communicate their attitudes toward each other, toward the Bible, toward God, toward prayer, toward church, and toward neighbors. Attitudes form the atmosphere in which the child learns about people and how he should think about those people. *Everything parents say or imply about Scripture contributes to their children's attraction or aversion to biblical truth.*

Parenthood stirs up both enormous responsibility and great joy. It requires that best attention we can offer to make sure that the home into which we bring our children is ready for them spiritually, emotionally, physically, economically, socially, and in every other way. Remember the formula: first godly people, then godly partners, then godly parents.

Jean and Jack are students. No, they're not enrolled in any formal educational institution, but every day God is teaching them more about applying His truth to all three areas of their lives. They realize the impact of the world and its potential to disintegrate the Christian family, and they intend to win their spiritual battles as people, partners, and parents.

The day our son's pet dog accidently strangled herself brought sadness for the entire family. Oh, yes, we all loved that dog, but, more important, we loved our son, and he was hurting. He blamed himself for putting her on a choker chain before we went to church.

After giving Jeff some time to grieve in private, we talked of our loving God who had given us Spooky to enjoy for a time. We talked of the fact that God controls all life and death. God used those tender, teachable moments to bring our family closer as we shared that sad experience.

Questions for Discussion

1. How can a Christian couple prepare for the first child? What attitudes and habits should be cultivated?
2. What is your position on the use of contraceptives? Some Christians favor their use; some oppose. What are the arguments on each side?
3. What do we mean when we say "every child is different," and what application might that principle have in your family at this time?
4. In what specific ways does a baby learn love, trust, and security in his home?
5. How great is the problem of grandparents' "spoiling" young children, and what can parents do about it?

5

Precious Preschool Years

Bob and Lillie are the parents of three preschoolers—Bobby, Jr., is four, Carrie is two, and Ann just turned six months. Both parents love the Lord and have a deep desire to train their children in the truth of His Word. However Bob is feeling great pressures at his job. He works for a small but growing company whose future potential rests largely on its young executives. As vice president of sales, Bob takes advantage of seminars, extra work assignments, and frequent out of town trips.

Lillie struggles with her feelings about Bob's job. On one hand, she resents his obsession with work. Yet she knows there never seems to be enough money to pay the bills, and the expectations of higher pay each year as Bob climbs the corporate ladder tend to make the future look brighter. She feels trapped both in the system and in the house, surrounded by dirty diapers, crying children, broken toys, and all too frequent squabbles.

As the pressure builds, neither Bob nor Lillie like what they see happening to themselves or to their children, but so far there appears to be no escape.

A recent study conducted by the Washington University School of Medicine in St. Louis and funded by the National Institutes of Mental Health sought to gain new insights into the kinds of stress most damaging to children. Researchers focused primarily on family stress and emphasized that marital discord and psychiatric problems among parents tend to produce behavioral problems in young children. That information is not particularly new but confirms something we already know: parenting is more difficult in a high stress society.

In another article, however, Rodney Clapp describes one of America's most vulnerable abuse groups.

> There are many signs that children are increasingly less appreciated in our society and that childhood as we know it is threatened with change to the point of extinction. The boundary protecting children is no concrete, biological wall, as unchallengeable as the law of gravity. It is a thin, cultural veil, gradually raised in the past for good reason. It tears easily. And anyone who listens can hear it ripping.[1]

Statistics on child abuse are virtually impossible to tabulate accurately because so many cases go unreported and undetected. The most conservative figures we have show some 1.8 million children abused annually, with two thousand killed in the process. Those statistics hardly take into consideration the thousands of cases of emotional abuse. Even if we dilute the data as much as we can, we develop a picture of a nation killing its own children at the rate of six a day. And the most seriously abused children are preschoolers. How essential to hear again the words of our Lord: "And whoever welcomes a little child like this in my name welcomes me. But if anyone causes one of these little ones who believe in me to sin, it would be better for him to have a large millstone hung around his neck and to be drowned in the depths of the sea" (Matthew 18:5-6).

1. Rodney Clapp, "Vanishing Childhood," *Christianity Today*, May 18, 1984, pp. 12-19.

NEEDS OF PRESCHOOL CHILDREN

"No discipline seems pleasant at the time, but painful. Later on, however, it produces a harvest of righteousness and peace for those who have been trained by it" (Hebrews 12:11).

There is no comparable period of life during which a person learns more and progresses more rapidly than the three years immediately prior to entering school. It is *the* time when parents have their greatest opportunity to determine the values and life-style of their children.

How would you help Bob and Lillie think through their parental priorities, particularly with a focus on the needs of preschoolers? Let's consider five crucial areas.

PHYSICAL NEEDS

Our children have many complex needs during the important preschool years. Serious parents will face earnestly the issue of nutrition, recognizing that only a healthy child can be a truly happy child. And the Bible makes Christian parents responsible for their children's physical well-being. Paul wrote to Timothy, "Anyone who won't care for . . . those living in his own family, has no right to say he is a Christian" (1 Timothy 5:8, TLB).

Passages like that make Bob realize that earning money to support his family can be defended biblically as well as socially. But he wonders whether "providing," even in the area of physical needs, means more than just bringing home enough money? Children need to learn how to throw a ball, ride a bike, or climb a tree. How will Bob's money help them do that? In what ways can he *provide* as a godly father?

There is an obvious link between health and discipline in the home. Preventive measures include orderly eating with special emphasis on mealtime behavior, moderation in between-meal snacks, and the eating of healthy foods. Satisfying physical hunger plays a significant training role in the Christian home.

MENTAL NEEDS

God also expects us to satisfy our children's mental hunger. Preschool children overflow with questions provoked by the everyday experiences of life. Some of the questions seem foolish to adults, and their number seems endless. Careful parent-teachers, however, see teachable moments arising out of those questions. The wonderful spirit of inquiry that God has given children is designed to produce learning in the informal and natural setting of the home. We still live under the challenge Moses once gave to Israel: "The secret things belong to the Lord our God, but the things revealed belong to us and to our children forever, that we may follow all the words of this law" (Deuteronomy 29:29).

Many times Lillie tires of hearing questions such as, "What's that?" "How does this work?" "What are you doing?" "Can I help?" She has several options. She can ignore the questions, she can scold the children for asking, she can answer briefly, or she can see each question as an opportunity to teach her children an important value of life.

But remember that preschool children have no sense of abstract understanding. They depend upon sensory experiences to relay information to the mind. That is why good Sunday school lessons use a fuzzy piece of cotton for a lamb's tail or perfume on the blotter picture of a flower. It also explains why moms and dads should create "make and do" learning opportunities for children in this age bracket whether they are involved in creative story-telling, collecting items from nature, or developing an appreciation for God's world.

Remember too that during the preschool years it is essential to establish the authority and control of parents as the child's most important teachers—a position we must never surrender until they become adults.

EMOTIONAL NEEDS

Little Carrie has begun to kick anything in her path whenever her parents or older brother don't let her have her way. Bob and Lillie could attribute her behavior to the fact that she is in the "terrible twos" and assume she will soon grow out of that phase. Or they might discover that Carrie is acting out of sinful defiance despite her tender age (Psalm 51:5). Whatever their cause, young children's emotions are intense and cannot be ignored.

During the impressionable early years, children usually demonstrate a high level of emotional hunger. Confidence in the love and acceptance of their parents is essential to healthy psychological adjustment. Sometimes we think "superiority" over our children is maintained by force. Actually, a climate of constant friction eats away at the very relationships we want to build.

Naturally, inconsistency or careless indulgence are just as harmful as harshness. Children must understand the ground rules for the home in which they live and respond accordingly. *Discipline is much more than punishment; it provides order and system in the home.* When that order is defied or disturbed, punishment must be the result. Love demands a willingness to take the switch in hand when necessary to protect the integrity of the training process. Preschool children should not be allowed to:

- Defy the commands of parents by words or behavior
- Interrupt conversations of adults
- Take the initiative in family decisions without permission (e.g., changing channels on the TV set, refusing to eat food put before them, and so on)
- Combat parental decisions by argument, back-talk, or temper tantrums

Preschool years are not too early to activate the implications of Samuel's warning to Saul: "For rebellion is like the sin of divination, and arrogance like the evil of idolatry. Because you have rejected the word of the Lord, he has rejected you as king" (1 Samuel 15:23).

SOCIAL NEEDS

A child's social hunger must be met by conscientious parents. A preschool child who learns to relate to other children will undergo less culture shock when he or she enters school. Having brothers or sisters helps the process of socialization, but a child must also learn to relate to peers outside of his family. Too many children, even in Christian homes, tend to focus upon themselves. Once an attitude of selfishness and egotism develops, you'll find it hard to break.

A family we know keeps a jar of cookies available to the children in an attempt to teach them to share. The parents have decided that the distribution of only one or two cookies to each child at snack time will make them covetous of their own things. If there are always plenty of cookies, however, they will feel free to give to others, confident that they will still have enough.

But such a plan is self-defeating. In the first place, everything is not so amply available that we can always have as much as we wish. Second, sharing does not mean giving with assurance that you will not be deprived, but giving something of your own. How much better to give those children two to four cookies each, asking them to share equally with the friends with whom they are playing. Teach them the biblical principle so earnestly followed by the early church: "All the believers were one in heart and mind. No one claimed that any of his possessions was his own, but they shared everything they had" (Acts 4:32).

SPIRITUAL NEEDS

Finally, it is the privilege of the Christian parent to satisfy the spiritual hunger of the preschool child. The Bible demands just three things of children: honor of parents, obedience to parents (Ephesians 6:1), and a return on parental investment (1 Timothy 5:4). If we as parents do not insist on the fulfilling of those simple qualifications, we have sinned against our children and against God.

Teaching and training (making the child obedient to orders) are both essential ingredients in meeting the child's spiritual needs. We instruct our little ones in the basic truths of God's Word and help them to live orderly lives conditioned by faith, love, obedience, and respect. Those wonderful ingredients are interwoven into a seamless garment of home life.

Parents should begin during those early preschool years to teach God as a vital part of all of life. A child can soon realize that God has make the furry kitten, the good-smelling flowers, and the cold milk. Parents quick to make their child aware of things around him will enable him to realize that all good things come from God. That realization will take the child another step toward the ultimate, vital relationship with God that we desire for him (Psalm 78:1-6).

Here Bob and Lillie need to do some serious rescheduling. They will not *find* time to accomplish the spiritual goals in their family; they will have to *make* time. Knowing that it should happen, wishing that it would happen, or even planning that someday it might happen will not get the job done. They need to *make* it happen, and they need to make it happen *now*.

NURTURING PRESCHOOL CHILDREN

Nurturing—a wonderful term commonly used in the botanical realm and more recently carried over to describe what happens to children in the physical family and new believers in the spiritual family. It describes constant care with an emphasis on feeding, shading, pruning, and developing plants and people through meticulous and patient care. That's exactly what Christian parents do during those all important first five years in the lives of their children. Here are some of the requirements of nurturing.

EXAMPLE

Children are incurable mimics. When he was just five or six years old we noticed our son in our bedroom spending some time looking at himself in the mirror. Since that behavior was rather unusual for a boy his age Dad waited to see what would happen next. Soon the question on his mind came tumbling out: "Dad, do I look as much like you as people say I do?" Upon being assured that the assessment of friends and neighbors was accurate, he concluded: "I'm going to follow you around wherever you go so that when I'm older I'll look even more like you than I do now."

Preschool children may not always say it quite that way, but they believe it, and in most cases that's precisely the behavioral result. Consider these words by Fred Brock:

> A careful man I ought to be,
> A little fellow follows me.
> I do not dare to go astray,
> For fear he'll go the self same way.
> I cannot once escape his eyes,
> What 'ere he sees me do he tries.
> Like me he says he's going to be—
> The little chap that follows me.
> He thinks that I am good and fine,
> Believes in every word of mine.
> The base in me he must not see—
> The little chap that follows me.
> I must remember as I go,
> Through summer's sun and winter's snow.
> I'm building for the years to be—
> That little chap who follows me.

SECURITY

Children must feel they are wanted and welcome in their homes. At a young age, they can feel safe in a strange and changing world only when they know that, despite their mistakes, their parents will continue to love and help them. The Christian family should discuss spiritual things naturally, just as naturally as they discuss the weather, school activities, or events around the house. Family worship ought also to be a normal and common behavior, not some ritual superimposed upon the real life of the family. Spiritual nurturing takes place in a spiritual atmosphere of family unity.

DISCIPLINE

By discipline we mean an ordered, structured pattern of family life in which each child knows precisely what is expected of him and what will happen if he fails to meet those expectations. Discipline provides security, an essential element of nurturing.

TEACHING

Urie Brofenbrenner once wrote that American families tend to create an emotional vacuum that is not filled by American schools. He warns that too many Americans worry about their children and too few really care for them and teach them, and he urges us to provide character education at home.[2]

The Bible depicts the home as a school in which children learn (2 Timothy 3:15). Sunday schools are important. Camps are important. Parachurch ministries are important. But the primary teaching agency (especially for preschool children) is the home.

COOPERATION

Family living requires teamwork, and the team leaders have to think alike on crucial issues. Even if a specific event seems to produce disagreement, Mom and Dad need to publicly support each other's commands, rules, and discipline. Disagreements on family policies and decisions should be discussed, of course, but away from the presence of the children. The children need to see love and mutual respect between the parents and among all members of the family.

2. Urie Brofenbrenner, *Two Worlds of Childhood* (New York: Russell Sage Foundation, 1969).

NEWNESS OF PRESCHOOL CHILDREN

Special joys come into parents' lives when new babies arrive. Few experiences in life compare to the knowledge that God's beautiful gift resulted from the expression of love between his parents. But the joys are accompanied by new pressures that call for special adjustments.

CONSIDER YOUR PRIORITIES

Burton White, at the Center for Parent Education in Newton, Massachusetts, claims his research confirms that the educational consequences of the first three years of life contribute heavily to lifelong development. So why do increasing numbers of young parents who claim to be Christians and understand the biblical demands of parenting allow others to care for and control their children during those crucial early years?

Your child's development should be one of your highest priorities. Who will have the joy of seeing all the wonderful firsts unfolding during those early years? Who will hear his first prayer—his parents or his baby-sitter? Who will formulate his values—his parents or the director of the day care center? The years of unspeakable joy for parents can only be fully appreciated when the child is a priority.

ASSUME CONTROL

Parental authority is a crucial issue for the Christian family. It may be the watershed that divides the genuinely evangelical viewpoint on the family from that of those uncertain about the authority of Scripture. Parents are certainly not perfect, but they are expected by the Heavenly Father to assume control over the behavior of their children, particularly during these preschool years when "instant obedience" must be developed.

TAKE TIME

Nurturing takes place naturally in the daily experiences of family life, but some specific formalities can be built into the system. For example, keep at least one night of the week free for being with the family (a minimal goal). We often hear about quality time, a phrase that might often be an escape clause for moms or dads who are gone too often. The phrase, however, can legitimately mean valuing the hours we do have and trying to show our children that we really want to be with them even when we can't.

KEEP YOUR MINISTRY LIFE IN BALANCE

Christian parents need to say *no* to ministry overload. Yes, every Christian ought to be involved and active in some way at his church, but that's no excuse for rushing out three or four nights a week and burning up hours that should be spent at home in parental ministry. Some Christian parents involve themselves in so many church activities and programs that they don't have time to carry on the primary responsibilities God has given them at home.

PAY ATTENTION TO SPECIAL TIMES

One time Dad took our daughter to a Kiwanis luncheon when Mom was not able to go, and it was the highlight of her week if not her month. Not only that, it really meant something to the Kiwanians as a visible demonstration of a father-daughter relationship. Family projects, hobbies, neighborhood events, church events, and even just working around the house can all be made into special times.

Don't forget family vacations, an important time to build family unity. If you can, set aside at least one time during the year when the entire family can be together and apart—together with each other and apart from other people, telephones, television, and everything that tends to confuse our lives and drive wedges between us.

About ten years ago, Ann Landers took a survey asking a singular question: "If you had it do over again, would you have children?" Ten thousand women answered. Seventy percent said they would not. According to the columnist, the negative mail fell into four major categories.

1. Young parents who were deeply concerned about global hunger, overpopulation, and the possibility that we might incinerate ourselves with nuclear weapons
2. Parents who claimed that their children had ruined their marriage
3. Older parents whose children had grown up and left home and for all practical purposes, abandoned their families
4. Bitter parents whose teenagers were in trouble

Interpreting their responses Ann raised the question about whether answers would have been different twenty years earlier. She concluded, "While it is true that children have rebelled against parents from time immemorial (rebellion is a normal symptom of growing up and achieving independence), never in the history of our country have the rebellious young managed to generate so much bitterness and total alienation."[3]

The Bible has an answer to the problem of those seven thousand women who would not have children if they had it to do over again. We have described it as a biblical program of love and nurture in the Christian home—and it begins during those precious preschool years.

Questions for Discussion

1. In addition to the needs of preschool children suggested by the authors, what others could be named?
2. How can parents create questions in the minds of their children and then design teaching situations to answer those questions?

3. Ann Landers, "If You Had It to Do Over Again—Would You Have Children?" *Good Housekeeping*, June 1976, pp. 100-101.

3. Name some family situations that might create insecurity and confusion in a young child's life, then describe how they could be avoided or alleviated.
4. Does the Bible really suggest that parents use physical punishment? How are we to understand such verses in Proverbs?
5. How do you feel about mothers of preschool children working? What are the alternatives?
6. At what point should rigorous enforcement of family rules begin (such as finishing meals, going to bed on time, and so on), and what kinds of punishment would be effective for enforcing them?

6

Energy, Enthusiasm, and Elementary School

Wearing his brand new clothes and carrying a shiny lunch pail, little Jimmy walked up the steps of the schoolhouse. On the top step he turned, with a big smile waved good-bye to Mommy, and entered for the first time his new world of chalkboards, books, teachers, and new friends.

Jimmy couldn't see the tears in his mother's eyes as she turned to go back home. Nor could he understand that life in their family would never be quite the same. He would be spending as many as thirty hours a week away from the family. He would develop a love for his teacher that could become competitive. And soon he would be challenging Mother on occasion by saying, "But my teacher said—"

Although he is now going to school all day and his world is expanding rapidly, his parents still represent the most important influence in Jimmy's life.

This chapter will focus on children six through eleven. In a day when 55 percent of all children in America have two parents who work outside the home, and in which many others live in single parent households with one parent who works, understanding and developing relationships with elementary children is foundational to effective family life.

New Fun—New Frustration

Jimmy will be a different boy when he comes home from school that first day, and the difference will increase with each day he spends in a diverse kind of social network—meeting new children and adults, doing new things, and sensing a decreasing dependence upon his parents.

LEARNING NEW RELATIONSHIPS

As parents, we are required to fulfill many different roles and responsibilities in the lives of our children. One important role is that of a *servant*. That may not sound very glamorous until we realize that Jesus said, "Whosoever will be chief among you, let him be your servant" (Matthew 20:27, KJV*).

The opportunities to serve are countless. There are always clothes to be washed, meals to prepare, a bicycle to fix, a bruised knee to care for, or a runny nose to wipe. Those responsibilities should never be considered inconveniences but rather opportunities to share with and care for our children.

Parents also serve as leaders. We serve as the source for physical characteristics, attitudes, convictions, and the value system that will form their lives. When we're spiritually out of tune, our children will be quick to detect and copy the sour notes.

Perhaps a parent's most important role elevates him or her to *teacher*. A child's lifetime exposes him to teachers, but none will be as important as his own parents. We may get a lot of help from Sunday school, children's church, school, clubs, and other agencies, but the responsibility for each child's education rests upon the shoulders of his parents.

Sometimes Christian parents are guilty of being concerned only that their children accept Christ as Savior. Secular education is turned over to the state and Christian training to the church. We must be sure that our children are taught the *entire* Bible "for teaching, rebuking, correcting and training in righ-

*King James Version.

teousness, so that the man of God may be thoroughly equipped for every good work" (2 Timothy 3:16-17).

LEARNING NEW RESPONSIBILITIES

Soon Jimmy will blossom as he learns to read about exciting adventures, to write his thoughts on paper, to develop musical skills, or to participate in games and sports. In some of those areas he may experience failure. In fact, keen competition and the lack of acceptance by peers will offer challenging areas that Jimmy will find difficult to handle.

As the maturing child takes on school and social responsibilities and becomes more independent, parents still meet many basic needs. A secure child relaxes in confident affection. He knows he is loved and wanted at home. Parents demonstrate their love in many small ways such as interest in school work and extracurricular activities. We agree with Dr. Haim Ginott: "It is desirable that the mother be at home to greet her child upon his return from school." Parents should notice and enjoy the things their children are making, doing, learning, and reading.

Children also need a sense of approval. They must understand that they really belong in the family because the way they feel about themselves depends upon relationship to other family members. Emphasize successes; minimize failures.

Young children learn many new responsibilities as they expand their relationships. A seven year-old, for example, must be able to get along not only with his parents, brothers, and sisters, but also school friends, neighborhood friends, and teachers. Christ's teachings tell us about love, kindness, sharing, tenderness, goodness, meekness, and many other Christian attributes. Godly parents would like to see those attitudes exemplified in their children. How can they make sure that will happen? Will children automatically respond because we tell them to or because they know what Jesus said? Perhaps two areas of home training point most directly to those questions.

Self-concept is an important element in the way a child behaves. Psychologist Bruce Narramore writes, "All of our behavior is guided by our self-esteem. When a child thinks he is a 'bad' boy, he will probably act that way." Obviously, it is not helpful for parents to constantly criticize, ridicule, and tear down.

Discipline is another way parents can help their children achieve biblical standards. An orderly home spells out acceptable and unacceptable behavior. When children know the limits and what will happen if the rules are broken, they can learn to respond accordingly. Of course, parents must be consistent in coming through with the punishment when the limits for acceptable behavior are broken.

So much crucial learning takes place during these years. The child's academic accomplishments alone are fantastic. Many nonreaders become prolific readers. This age group learns math concepts, science, spelling, and manuscript as well as cursive writing.

LEARNING NEW SOCIAL BEHAVIORS

Closely tied to cognitive learning situations (knowledge) are corresponding social behaviors. Common courtesy does not come automatically to young children. Selfishness comes from original sin. Children want people to stop and listen whenever they have something to say. Too often they forget to say "thank you," "please," and "excuse me." When we practice politeness and respect for each other and our children, these qualities will slowly develop in their lives.

Dinner is over, but Jimmy's family sits a few minutes longer to share the events of the day. All of a sudden Jimmy pipes up, "May I be excused?" Mom and Dad look at each other in stunned disbelief before Dad finally responds, "Yes; yes, you may. Thank you for asking." Jimmy pushes his chair away from the table and leaves.

Why now? After weeks or months of trying to elicit that minor expression of politeness, why does he finally come out with it? Jimmy was simply practicing new social skills, testing his parents' reaction. Obviously praise and positive reinforcement are essential—especially the first few times a child responds in ways in which parents have been encouraging him to act.

Every child needs many opportunities to be with companions his own age, to gain confidence in his own personality and the ability to make friends and get along well with others. He needs to learn to give and take, sharing some of his own possessions. The child who knows the feeling of belonging to the family team will be concerned about being a representative of the family in society.

NEW CHALLENGES—NEW CHAOS

Ray and Kay are ten-year-old twins. Mrs. Stevens, their mother, is very frustrated about their behavior patterns. They have always been fairly close and enjoyed each other's company. But now it seems that Ray thinks all girls are stupid (especially his sister), and Kay thinks all boys are big pests (especially her brother). When not fighting about something, they seem to spend their time giggling.

Add to this compatibility problem the problem of messiness. Ray always looks like a mess and doesn't seem to care. His room lies in shambles. Kay is not much better. Each child's room contains evidence of the beginnings of many collections: rocks, a box of dead insects, baseball cards, and coins stuffed into a drawer.

What great tragedy has befallen the Stevens' home? The only problem is that there are two very active, normal ten-year-olds living there, and Mrs. Stevens must learn to understand them. Is it inevitable that children must constantly fight in the chaotic arena of their rooms? No, of course not, but they will at times.

HARNESSING CHILDHOOD ENERGY

The later elementary years of childhood stand out as some of the most delightful. Full of energy and usually very healthy, children enter all kinds of activities with enthusiasm and interest, especially exploring and investigating. At this age they have deep feelings of love toward family members and friends even though they may find it difficult to express them. Boys especially find it easier to write notes or make something for a parent, brother, sister, or friend.

One day our nine-year-old daughter wrote a note to her twelve-year-old brother and said, "I love you, Jeff." At the bottom he wrote, "I love you too," and returned the note. The initial effort was elaborately prepared and probably motivated as an antidote to a little quarrel. The curt response was sincere, but the typical emotionless reply of a junior high boy.

How does knowing all this help us solve the problems in the home? Mr. and Mrs. Stevens want Ray and Kay to be willing to take responsibility for their own actions. They're hoping for less fighting, neater rooms, and quick obedience to their commands, to say nothing of accountability for schoolwork.

In actuality, the Stevenses have been building relationships and understanding during the preschool and early elementary years. Now they can build on a good foundation of respect and consistency, making the job much easier.

Not all types of control require anger or nagging. James Dobson, in *Dare to Discipline*, suggests positive reinforcement such as money, gifts, or a special privilege of some kind. Bruce Narramore's helpful book *Help, I'm a Parent* offers many different approaches. One of the suggestions is called "natural consequences."

Let's take Ray's cluttered room. Ray goes into his room to search for a library book that is due the next day—a mission impossible. Mom's natural response may be to sort through things while complaining, "If you'd keep your room in order like I've told you to, you'd be able to find things." How much better for her to allow Ray to take responsibility for the situation himself. He'll soon learn that it's hard to find things in a disorderly room.

If he doesn't find the book, he should pay the late fee or the price of the book from his own money. In that way, he will learn a great deal more about responsibility than he would if Mother found the book or Dad gave him the money to pay for the book.

HOBBIES AND HEROES

In Colossians 3:17 Paul tells us, "Whatever you do, whether in word or deed, do it all in the name of the Lord Jesus, giving thanks to God the Father through him."

In a Christian family, should we expect children's hobbies, interests, collections, and heroes to be different from those of their non-Christian friends? If they are not, there may be something wrong in our homes.

Children in later elementary years emerge as eager collectors and hero worshipers. Parents can help channel those interests into meaningful learning experiences. Studies from nature increase your child's appreciation for the God Who created them. Buy a book about shells or rocks, and then plan a family trip to the beach or the park so your child can see that you are genuinely interested in his interests.

What about heroes? Too often the heroes are rock singers or TV stars. Parents can channel the hero craze by supervising closely what their children watch on television and listen to on the radio. Make available good Christian books, fiction as well as nonfiction. Set aside a certain block of time each week for reading. *The Family Bible Library,* by V. Gilbert Beers, portrays in a beautiful way the marvelous biblical stories featuring the Lord as the primary hero.

HANDLING JUNIOR JUSTICE

Parents of a junior child (grades 4-6) hear one complaint over and over again: "That's not fair." Junior justice is important whether in games or as punishment for wrongdoing. So it becomes even more important for parents to discuss (in private) the rules of the house and then be sure all members of the family understand them.

Often during these years children begin to challenge their mothers and will obey their dads more quickly. Dad's leadership must affirm and reinforce the validity of Mother's authority.

Our children must realize that we parents are not perfect. We sin and need to ask God for forgiveness. And let's not be ashamed to ask our children to forgive us when we act unjustly or are unkind toward them.

NEW PRINCIPLES—NEW PROBLEMS

All parents will probably face one or more of the following problems while rearing their children. But a family that is saturated with love will find the solutions to the problems more quickly than one in which little or no love is shown.

An article by Jeannette Acrea in *Psychology for Living* tells of a girl named Judy who was hurt very deeply and eventually needed psychotherapy because her mother and father loved each other so much they found very little time for her. She felt left out, unimportant, and unnoticed.[1]

In healthy families children need to see their parents express love for each other, but children must also be held, hugged, kissed, and told of the parents' love for them.

There are other ways of showing love besides physical contact. We show love by playing, by doing things with our children, by talking, reading, or just sitting quietly together.

TIMIDITY AND FEAR

Mary is a shy and fearful child, afraid of any new situations. Her fear involves the dark, storms, and animals. Often she wants to sleep with her parents or cries uncontrollably. Al-

1. Jeannette Acrea, "Daddy Look at Me," *Psychology for Living*, June 1972, p. 13.

though her parents may try to reason with her, talking probably will not change the situation.

Fear need not be bad. Because fire, deep water, or a busy street can hurt a child, we must teach him to have a certain amount of fear. But some parents instill unwarranted fear into a child unknowingly, either by their own phobias or by their actions and comments.

Fear is a learned emotion. A child accumulates fear from contact with other people. Consequently, we can also teach him *not* to have fear. The book *Living with Children*, by Gerald R. Patterson and M. Elizabeth Guillion, offers several good suggestions for dealing with frightened children. One example: train your child to decrease his fear with positive reinforcers.

Let's consider Mary's fear of animals. We can teach Mary that gentle treatment of a kitty reduces the need to be afraid. When the kitty comes into the room, we help Mary remain calm by allowing her to observe it from a distance without becoming frightened and crying. Then we reward that behavior with praise. But if Mary begins to scream, the worst thing her mother can do is take Mary into her arms to comfort her. That reinforces the precise behavior she is trying to extinguish. Gradually, Mary might be able to touch the kitty and later hold the kitty. Don't force such behavior too quickly, and reward each level of achievement with praise.

The loving Christian parent can also give strength to his child from the Word of God. The child can begin to understand the depth of God's love and promises such as "There is no fear in love. But perfect love drives out fear, because fear has to do with punishment. The man who fears is not made perfect in love" (1 John 4:18). Then soon we will begin to see victory over fear.

HYPERACTIVITY

Perhaps you've been thinking that "shy, retiring, and fearful" certainly does not describe your children. Noisy, loud, and full of exuberance would be more like it. Maybe there never seems to be enough peace and quiet around the house.

David never sits when he can stand, never stands when he can walk, never walks when he can run, and never runs when he can sprint. His arms and legs seems to be a perpetual motion machine, a human windmill without direction or purpose. His mouth is an irresistible force, operating non-stop during waking hours and frequently interrupting others without discriminating between family, friends, and strangers.

All children are active in varying degrees just because they are children. Parents must allow for a certain amount of rough and tumble play. The key is that children learn the proper place and time for boisterous play.

Agree on a punishment when the rule is broken and a reward when the rule is remembered. Then carry out the plan. Remember hyperactivity *might* have a neurological cause, so a medical examination is usually a wise investment.

Our daughter Julie was a hyperactive child needing medication for a period of time. It would have been easy for us to excuse any improper behavior as a result of her hyperactivity. However, we determined to make few exceptions and expect compliance to family rules despite temporary minor disability. By balancing love, firmness, and consistency we watched our daughter move from parent-control to self-control and eventually to consciously given Spirit-control.

REBELLION

When a child becomes extremely aggressive, destructive, or rebellious, professional help is needed. Those may be symptoms of a deeper problem, and parents should act accordingly to help the child find answers to his anxieties.

Parents face other problems that could come under the general category of specific sins. The Bible speaks strongly about such things as lying, stealing, anger, and jealousy. In Ephesians 4:25-28 we read,

Therefore each of you put off falsehood and speak truthfully to his neighbor for we are all members of one body. "In your anger do not sin." Do not let the sun go down while you are still angry, and do not give the devil a foothold. He who has been stealing must steal no longer, but must work, doing something to share with those in need.

The child who consistently lies, steals, or displays outbursts of anger must be made to realize the seriousness of his behavior, not only in the eyes of his parents, but also in the eyes of God.

Because God knows that children are born with a sinful nature and find it easier to sin than to do what pleases Him, He gives them parents. And He tells those parents what to do:

> The rod of correction imparts wisdom, but a child left to itself disgraces his mother. When the wicked thrive, so does sin, but the righteous will see their downfall. Discipline your son, and he will give you peace; he will bring delight to your soul. (Proverbs 29:15-17)

Recent research reported in *The Atlantic Monthly* describes a major problem in American homes today—many parents simply do not know how to rear their children. The problem is caused not so much by neurosis or indifference as by plain old-fashioned incompetence. Researcher Gerald Patterson at the Oregon Social Learning Center claims his studies indicate a child may misbehave because his parents "fail to tell him clearly how he is expected to behave, fail to monitor his behavior closely to insure that he behaves that way, and fail to enforce the rules with appropriate rewards and penalties, promptly, and unambiguously delivered."[2]

Answers do not come easily for any of the behavioral problems we face with our children. But Christian parents can claim

---

2. James Q. Wilson, "Raising Kids," *The Atlantic Monthly*, October 1983, p. 52.

the guidance and instruction of the Holy Spirit. As we allow Him to control our lives, He will lead us into all truth.

Questions for Discussion

1. How can Christian parents prepare an elementary child for the relationships and problems he will face in the wider social world?
2. In what ways can Christian parents exert greater influence over their children in either public or private school settings?
3. What effect does a mother's influence have on the life of a young child?
4. Identify several specific ways in which parents can show love to their children.
5. If one parent is not a Christian, what can be done to increase consistency and cooperation in child care?

7

Early Teen Years: Doorway to Independence

Kevin Duncan is thirteen and proud to be a teenager. He sees his newly acquired status as a major step toward adulthood and the elusive dream of running his own life. And in our society, he is right. Responsibility for one's own affairs has been steadily moving into lower age levels.

But Kevin has a problem. Well, really, two problems—Mr. Duncan and Mrs. Duncan. You see, Kevin is their only child, and, in their opinion, he's just growing up too fast. Somehow they can't adjust their view of Kevin from child to young man. Their relationship with their son strains at what he thinks are restrictive limits on his life. He often complains to his parents, "Stop treating me like a baby."

The Duncans tend to think of the passage from dependence to independence as an *event,* which they expect to coincide with Kevin's graduation from high school. But maturity is not an *event*—it is a *process*. And parents should begin that process early in childhood and bring it to a happy climax (as far as their part is concerned) somewhere in the late teens or early twenties. Perhaps we could diagram the process like this:

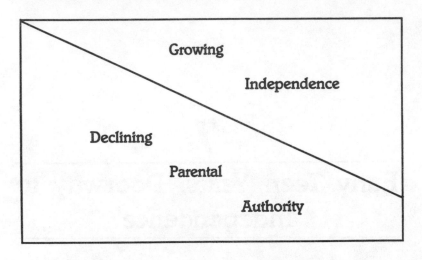

Notice that the diagonal division line does not go all the way down to the baseline at adulthood. Infants are absolutely dependent, but adults are *not* absolutely independent. We should teach our teenagers to recognize independence as a relative and restricted commodity. A crucial biblical principle surfaces here—the dependence of all believers of any age on the Heavenly Father (2 Corinthians 3:5).

KEEPING THE CONFLICT LEVEL DOWN

KNOW YOUR CHILD

Although children at each age level exhibit certain general characteristics, every child is an individual. That leaves parents in need of two kinds of information to facilitate wise decision-making: knowledge of young teens generally and knowledge of our own children specifically.

How much freedom can we give young teens? How soon can it be given? What characteristics mark young teens (ages twelve to fourteen)?

Enthusiasm and energy are directed toward the peer group. Youth activities start at church, and elementary school has been left behind. Learning begins to take on more serious dimensions. Separate classrooms and different teachers for each course at school bring reminders of advancement.

Reasoning processes are taking hold. Whats give way to whys. With some junior high students the questions are kept in; with others they are openly voiced.

Girls have been maturing much more rapidly than boys, and the difference continues until the eighth or ninth grade when the boys begin to catch up.

But Mr. and Mrs. Duncan can only apply this data when they know where Kevin fits into his own age-group patterns. And, ironically, the way he acts and reacts at thirteen depends to a great extent upon the way his parents have treated him for the past thirteen years.

Mutual respect and trust rooted in love do not drop from the sky when a child turns thirteen, or sixteen, or twenty-one. They are carefully cultivated throughout the process of helping our children grow from dependence to independence. Far from being an absence of discipline and order, freedom is closely connected to both, in the family and in society. And with freedom comes risk. Not all the teens who are given a wide measure of independence by their parents prove deserving. But parents who want to see their young people become confident and mature Christians will take the risk.

KNOWING THE CAUSES OF CONFLICT

When Kevin and his parents start in on one of their frequent arguments, their family doesn't look or sound very Christian. Shouting, angry words, bitterness, and accusations precede pouting, hurt feelings, and the absence of visible love. How do these arguments start, and how can they be avoided? Family counseling experts tell us that several key conflict-points show up again and again.

Criticism. Kevin's parents repeatedly "hassle" him about his hairstyle, his music, and some of his friends. He responds with defensive and reactionary attitudes (Proverbs 23:24-25).

Poor communication. Most of the discussions in the Duncan household deal with trivial things. Kevin's personal problems and feelings have never been shared with his parents (Proverbs 19:20).

Disrespect and disobedience. During his earlier childhood years Kevin was not required to submit to his parents' will. Now his strong will displays itself in rebellion and defiance (Proverbs 17:2).

Inadequate self-concept. Kevin lacks confidence in himself and optimism about his life. Since Mom and Dad have always made most of the decisions, he never developed the assurance that he could think through issues for himself. Not having responsibilities around the house (Mom always did it all), Kevin hasn't felt important to the family (Proverbs 3:1-2).

Defensiveness. Mr. and Mrs. Duncan have heard about the difficulties of the teen years. And, having prepared themselves for turmoil, their expectations tend to create the problems. In an attempt to retain their authoritative roles, they seem hesitant to show respect for Kevin. They never apologize when wrong, nor do they ask Kevin's opinion on important family matters (Proverbs 20:11).

Teenagers need the family. The unity and security in the circle of love offers a sustaining refuge in the difficult changes young teens face. Parental models take on more meaning during these years as teens begin to understand some of the decisions Mom and Dad face and the reasons things must be run a certain way.

KNOWING HOW TO HANDLE TRANSITION

Parents need to recognize that their teenagers are products of their own cultural environments. In one sense our kids are not unique, because everyone passes through the teen years with their accompanying problems and blessings. In another sense they are unique, because they are the only generation facing the distinctive problems of this particular day. Teenagers growing up in the early forties grappled with the meaning and horror of World War II. Forty years later toxic waste, acid rain, international terrorism, and the threat of nuclear holocaust present problems never thought of just a generation and a half ago.

Nostalgia makes for happy family conversation but is usually useless as a tool for teaching or disciplining, because times tend to be so different. But biblical principles do not change, and they govern the relationship of teenagers to their parents in any age. The later verses of Luke 2 show the marvelous transition of Jesus from childhood to teen years. In verse 40 we see the shelter of the home providing a growth opportunity for the young child. As He became strong in spirit, filled with wisdom, and enjoyed the grace of God upon Him, Jesus went to Jerusalem with His parents for appropriate religious ritual.

Christian parents should see in this passage not only the vast wisdom of the twelve-year-old Son of God but also the frustration and confusion of parents who did not understand what He was trying to tell them and couldn't figure out why He behaved the way He did (v. 50). Quite simply, Mary and Joseph did not understand the transition of their emerging teenager. Sound familiar? Let's not minimize the agony, frustration, and perhaps even irritation in Mary's voice when she asked, "Son, why have you treated us like this? Your father and I have been anxiously searching for you!"

Verses 51 and 52 of the passage give us an important clue. Mary and Joseph, godly parents of the first rank, provided for their teenage son what Edith Schaeffer calls in one of her books "a control monitoring system." Jesus Christ, the Son of God, subjected Himself to His own parents at age twelve, and the passage seems to presume that the relationship continued into the teen years.

Having problems with your teenager? You can't go back and make him or her two years old again and start the process all over. You'll simply have to thrust yourself upon the grace of God and start fresh now. Admit your failures, open the lines of communication, show love in as many ways as possible, but never back off on that control monitoring system. Family unity and joy need not be disrupted or compromised just because those formerly docile, easily-managed little children have transformed themselves into questioning, confusing, challenging young teens.

GETTING SERIOUS ABOUT SEX EDUCATION

Through the emergence of new feelings, Kevin's body has been giving him clues that demonstrate his change into adolescence. Since he's always had a weak self-image, he struggles to accept the awkwardness, the change of pitch in his voice, and the constant signs of immaturity that seem to cause every girl he knows to tell him, "Grow up."

Since Kevin's parents have protected him and thought of him as their little boy, they have not really prepared him for the sexual changes taking place in his life. Like many other parents, they kept thinking there was plenty of time for those difficult discussions. But now his friends are talking constantly of their interest in girls, and he feels under pressure to experiment with some kind of sexual freedom.

Somehow Kevin desperately needs to understand that he belongs to God, who made him and loves him even as a clumsy adolescent boy. He must grasp a Christian view of human sexuality with its emphasis on restraint, respect, and reverence.

National rates for teenage pregnancies, births, and abortions stagger belief. In the mid-1980s 1 million American teenagers become pregnant each year and about 60 percent of those pregnancies result in live births. One percent terminate in miscarriages or stillbirths and 3 percent in abortion. To put it another way, nearly 10 percent of all American teenage girls become pregnant annually.

CONQUERING PARENTAL FEARS (TITUS 2:3-5)

Part of the problem with sex education is the negative sex role image presented by many parents. Recent research conducted by child psychiatrist Arthur Kornhaber suggests that more and more adolescents are becoming psychologically sabotaged by adults who really don't want to be parents themselves. Kornhaber complains, "Mothers who don't want to be mothers and 'liberated' women who feel their daughters ought not to learn feminine ways are robbing their daughters of their sexual identities. . . and the fathers by working too much and refusing to share their lives with their sons, are teaching these boys to retreat from their male responsibilities."[1]

The models Mom and Dad provide at home represent the most significant aspects of sex education, far more important than the content that will be taught in a course at school. Of course we are not suggesting that sex education begin only at age twelve or in the early teen years. Wise parents will carefully bring their children through a process of understanding sexuality from the earliest childhood years. But piercing questions and emerging adolescent physiology make this a crucial time for getting serious about sex education.

COMBATTING PERVERTED VIEWPOINTS (TITUS 2:11-14)

Homosexuality, transsexuality, premarital sexual promiscuity, and the general acceptance of recreational sex will make biblical sex education in the Christian home more difficult with each passing year. Christian parents must stand squarely on what Scripture says and avoid the confusion of the surrounding culture. Sex education gains meaning and strength only when based on the principle that marriage exists primarily for fellowship between the husband and the wife as a parallel to the communion between Christ and His church. We must make plain to our children that God has a name for sex outside of marriage—sin. Teach them that God wants us to enjoy sex —within marriage—as one of the good gifts He has given us.

CONSTRUCTING SEX EDUCATION ON SOLID THEOLOGY (TITUS 2:1, 6-8)

The Bible teaches absolute truth and a heavenly value system, both of which stand in stark contrast to the misguided eth-

1. Arthur Kornhaber, "Do Children Need Sex Roles?" *Newsweek*, June 10, 1974, p. 79.

ics of modern society. Any teaching that does not recognize all people as the creation of a sovereign, self-revealed God must at its very best offer a distorted view of sex and at its worst create a complete lack of sexual ethics. The job of sex education really doesn't belong to the school or the church, though both can help in some way. God has laid that burden squarely upon the shoulders of Christian parents.

So let's get with it, Mom and Dad. We can't be afraid of it; we've got to tackle it head-on and trust God to give us the courage and wisdom to do the job. Teaching is a major task of God's people, as Paul reminded Titus throughout the second chapter of that epistle. Take a moment to review the biblical guidelines articulated in the verses noted with each of the above points.

BEING WILLING TO ACCEPT ADOLESCENCE

The Anabaptists of the Reformation era designed an interesting plan for identifying the transition of persons from one stage of development to another. Their stages were essentially the same as ours—childhood, youth, and adulthood. They saw childhood as a stage of innocence and unself-willed development. At the first sign of action based on self-will the old Hutterites and other Anabaptists marked the beginning of "youth."[2]

ACCEPT GROWING INDEPENDENCE

In one sense the old Anabaptists locked themselves into good biblical theology. They argued that self-surrender, not self-development, is God's will, and we certainly have to agree with that. But modern research helps us understand the psychological make-up of young teens, and we can expect that growing independence depicted on the chart earlier in the chapter.

When Kevin comes to his parents to announce, "Some of my school friends are having a party and I want to go," their

2. David F. Tennant, "Anabaptist Theologies of Childhood and Education," *The Baptist Quarterly*, July 1984, pp. 310-11.

answer tends toward a flat yes or no. Instead, they need to give Kevin the opportunity to discuss the issues and have a voice in the choices that make up the maturing process. For example: Where is the party? Will there be any adult supervision? What other friends will be attending? What time will the party end? Is there any reason to think this might not be a good idea?

Parents who lead their young people through the decision-making process are not only helping them see why it is sometimes necessary to say no, but they are already preparing the next generation of parents and therefore perpetuating a Christian family beyond the boundaries of their own household.

Remember, children do not become independent at age twelve or fourteen or seventeen. They live in a constant state of maturation (growth) from the earliest childhood years on through adulthood. Successfully building a God-fearing family requires patience, diligence, and an understanding of foundational biblical principles, including the recognition of inevitable independence.

ACCEPT GROWING INTELLECT

A major step in a young teen's intellectual progress is the development of his ability to choose wisely between alternatives. True, it is not some shocking new responsibility that hits him when he passes twelve. It tends to show up in elementary school and junior high years as well. But the teen years bring a new level of decision-making—the spiritual, biblical process by which emerging teens are able to choose the right and reject the wrong because they have been given criteria for such choices over the past dozen years of their lives. Parents are responsible for seeing that children created in God's image reach their highest spiritual potential, appropriate God's wisdom and grace in making wise decisions, and become accountable for the outcomes of those decisions.

ACCEPT GROWING INCONSISTENCY

Our choice of the word *inconsistency* seems inconsistent. After all if the young teen is growing in independence and intelligence, should he not also be growing in consistency? Probably so if the environment around him would allow uninterrupted progress in social, emotional, and spiritual growth—but it does not. Peer pressure, confusion over self-esteem and importance in a group, and often the confusion of parental roles create inconsistent behavior baffling to parents and destructive to family relationships.

Our daughter, Julie, was still in junior high when she developed a friendship with another girl in our neighborhood. Several times the girl came to church with us, and then one day Julie asked if she could go to church with her new friend. We were extremely reluctant to let her go when we found out that the church was one we believed did not teach proper doctrine.

But after much discussion, we gave our consent. During the Sunday school class Julie engaged in a lengthy conversation with the teacher. As it turned out, her faith took a step forward because of her opportunity to defend the truth she had been taught at home from God's Word.

A Christian teenager attending a public school in which he encounters a blatantly pagan teacher receives a version of the world totally incompatible with what his parents have been teaching him for years. Who's right? His relatively uneducated parents, whose interests seem to him to be largely domestic or business related? Or this obviously brilliant teacher, who has given his life to the study of the information he presents in the classroom? It's easy to see how inconsistent thinking can arise.

Or perhaps two working parents who seem to have little time for the teens bring an inconsistency of values to the home. Earl Grollman and Gerri Sweder suggest ways to cut down on parent-generated confusion and inconsistency.[3]

3. Earl Grollman and Gerri Sweder, "Tips for Working Parents—From Kids," *Reader's Digest*, February 1986, pp. 107-10.

1. Discuss your work
2. Don't overwork
3. Don't come home grumpy
4. Don't go out too often
5. Listen to your child
6. Don't criticize unfairly
7. Start the day right
8. Make your home safe

To be sure, none of those can substitute for the presence of the parents themselves, but in today's world parenting may be the art of the possible rather than the ideal. And what makes it possible is the activating power of God's Spirit, who produces in us parental potential and guides our crucial decisions through prayer and obedience to God's Word (John 16:13-15).

Questions for Discussion

1. How can young teenagers really be made a part of family decisions?
2. How can parents meet and handle the problem of peer group influence?
3. In what ways can we make growing independence work for instead of against us as parents?
4. How can we help young teens adjust to the physical, sexual, and social changes of those years?
5. Think of the displaced children of the Bible (Joseph, Daniel, Daniel's three friends, Naaman's slave girl) most of whom were children or young teens at the time of their captivity. What do we see in their lives that teaches us something about the way they were taught at home?

8

Launching the Next Generation

An anonymous teenager, one among thousands of runaway young people today, wrote these words back home:

Dear Folks,

Thank you for everything, but I am going to Chicago and try and start some kind of a new life.

You asked me why I did those things and why I gave you so much trouble, and the answer is easy for me to give you, but I am wondering if you will understand.

Remember when I was just about six or seven and I used to want you to just listen to me? I remember all the nice things you gave me for Christmas and my birthday and I was really happy with the things—about a week—at the time I got the things, but the rest of the time during the year I really didn't want presents. I just wanted all the time for you to listen to me like I was somebody who felt things too, because I remember even when I was young, I felt things. But you said you were busy.

If anybody asks you where I am, tell them I've gone looking for somebody with time because I've got a lot of things I want to talk about.

Those are only selected paragraphs from a longer letter, but they represent a crucial problem in parent-teen relations today—misunderstanding. The term *generation gap* implies that this problem stems from the age difference between parents and their children. No doubt there are aspects of values and goals that do exaggerate varying attitudes between people in their teens and people in their thirties or forties. Pressures of the secular peer group make the teenagers of Christian parents think differently on some issues.

In today's confusing society teenagers strive to create a new set of values combining fragments of the traditional Protestant ethic, radical social movements of the early second half of the twentieth century, and the more recent affluent materialistic post-industrial society. According to famous pollster George Gallup,

> traditional values, such as greater respect for authority and more emphasis on closer family ties, have never been stronger among the country's teens. At the same time however teens also desire more emphasis in the future on greater self-expression, and the acceptance of sexual freedom. Technological progress traditionally has been respected in America, and although many young people rejected this concept in the 60s, technology now has won widespread acceptance among teens.[1]

Gallup surveyed teens thirteen to eighteen (this chapter concentrates on ages fifteen to twenty-one) and divided his findings according to sex and two age groupings, thirteen to fifteen and sixteen to eighteen. In the older grouping, 87 percent would welcome more emphasis on traditional family ties and 93 percent, more respect for authority.

Of course many questions cloud the research. Are the sampled teens representative of the national scene? Are their leanings toward authority brought about by fear of crime and terrorism rather than their own personal commitment to an orderly society? How do we harmonize such seemingly opposite

1. Robert Bezilla, "Teenagers Creating New Values for the Future," *Emerging Trends*, October 1985, p. 5.

commitments as emphasis on traditional family ties and more acceptance of sexual freedom? Problems like these are what make the later parenting years among the toughest. Like NASA crews, we stand around the shuttle eagerly but nervously awaiting lift-off.

COMMUNICATE

Things have not been going well in Eric Norton's life. It was as though a storm raged inside ready to overwhelm him at any moment. His parents, Paul and Joyce, felt totally helpless, as though they were observing the drama of their son's life from a distance.

Perhaps their greatest frustration came from knowing that parenting teens was not a new experience for them. Eric was the youngest of three, and the other two had made it through high school and off to college without any major disasters. Nor had Eric been a difficult child—always a good student, quiet, obedient, and consistently praised by his parents for his talents, grades, and whatever he excelled in, which was nearly everything he tried.

But for the past two months Paul and Joyce watched helplessly as their happy and well-adjusted teenager turned into a bitter, rebellious young man. His grades began to slip, he quit the basketball team, and his behavior toward home rules was best described as "totally careless." Earlier trust and open communication were gone, and the big task loomed large before them—how to reestablish a relationship with their own son.

Many needs of older teens are best met in a family context: patience and understanding regarding problems and changes; authority and controls to curb rebellion; security and love to combat the confusion and fear in society; and a place to belong and be affirmed during some tough years of one's life. Here's how we meet those needs.[2]

---

2. Cf. "Teenagers and Their Parents," in *The Family First* (Winona Lake, Ind.: BMH, 1979), p. 73.

DEVELOP A CLIMATE OF OPENNESS AND SINCERITY

Christian parents should be their teens' closest confidants and counselors. Yet too often church youth directors or high school guidance counselors preempt that role.

A recent survey conducted by columnist Jean Adams and published in *Parade*, offers some frightening insights.

- Teens believe they usually lose communication with their parents at age twelve.
- More than 90 percent said they prefer discussing their problems with their peers instead of with parents. Only 41 percent indicated a willingness to discuss serious problems with their fathers (and only 29 percent of the girls).
- Teens believe that most parents are not qualified to help with today's problems.

So much for the problems that many parents already know only too well. How can we cut the distance and span the communication gap? One way has already been mentioned: begin to build solid mutual trust relationships during the preschool years. Be a listener who can show genuine tolerance toward your teenager's peculiar ideas and flexibility to cope with his changing moods. Allow privacy, show respect, and spend time with him.

And remember that a climate of openness does not preclude standards of behavior, discipline, and even punishment. Those are all threads in the fabric of love and care that teens want no matter how overtly they seem to reject it. Parents must allow teens to move from dependence to independence in an orderly fashion without being constantly hassled.

BUILD A PROPER SELF-CONCEPT

Suicide statistics for American teenagers should shock us all. Adolescents attempt more than 12 percent of all suicides, and some reputable authorities suggest that teen suicide reports may be 50 percent understated because of a tendency to conceal the facts.

What do the unsuccessful suicide candidates say about why they did it? Here are some sample answers; notice how they all point to family deficiencies:

- Quarreling parents
- Conflict with parents, brother, or sisters
- Father or mother frequently absent from home
- Cruelty, rejection, or abandonment by parents
- Constant moving and changing houses and schools

Invariably these young people have a distorted view of themselves and their surroundings. Frustration turns to despair and attempts to find meaning in alcohol, drugs, or sex. Failing again, suicide seems the only alternative.

In the Christian home, parents can show their young people a depth of love and affection that draws them together to seek answers to life's complexities. Furthermore, they can show how God has designed for the indwelling Holy Spirit to produce love, joy, peace, and other spiritual fruit in the lives of believers (Galatians 5:22-23). These qualities are just the opposite of the alienation and futility they see around them.

With Memorial Day weekend just around the corner, Paul announced a family camping trip to a nearby state park. Eric's reaction was all too familiar and typical of his recent behavior—a silent walk to his room followed by a loud slam of the door. Without warning that evening at dinner Eric solemnly announced, "I'm not going camping; I have other plans." Paul was calm but refused to back away from what he thought should be a complete family project—Eric would go, and the matter was dropped.

Normally preparation for a Norton family camping trip involved the whole family. But not this time. The gloom of Eric's attitude hung heavily during the packing and driving, but somehow after arrival at the park and the arrangement of the camp site, the atmosphere began to change.

By the end of the weekend all three family members realized several important things. First, it had been a long time since they had taken time to just have fun together. Second, they were really listening to each other for a change, and somehow that was making a major difference in their relationship even over a short three-day period.

Eric admitted to spending time with a set of friends who involved him in a life-style he knew was not helping his Christian witness or spiritual growth. His parents listened intently and then frankly admitted they had contributed to the problem. How easy it had been to take Eric for granted—always the good kid. Assuming that they need spend no extra hours supervising this third child, they had become overly involved in their jobs, ministries at church, and other worthwhile causes in the community.

The weekend was only the beginning, but it was at least that. The storm in Eric's heart began to calm. Family communication had been rewound and reset like a spring-run clock, and that was a big first step.

TEACH CHRISTIAN VALUES

Jesus told us His followers would be misunderstood and hated by the world. Our goals, values, and life philosophies are opposite and conflicting.

Yet, peer popularity is a driving force in all teenagers, even those committed to Christ. Bucking the crowd is tough, and Christian teens need all the parental help they can get. Here are some sample issues in which Christian values stand in contrast to the contemporary standards of society:

> Biblical chastity versus recreational sex
> Biblical eternality versus worldly presentism
> Biblical absolutism versus secular relativism
> Biblical love versus passionate lust

The Christian answer to premarital sex is not, "You might get pregnant!" but, "Sex outside of marriage is sin." The argument against teenage marriage is not, "You can't afford to get married now—how will you support her?" but, "God's teaching about marriage shows us that such a serious step requires maturity and preparation."

Thank God for church, school, Christian friends, and any other positive influences on our young people. But the final source of understanding and security—and God's original plan—is still a close relationship between a teenager and his parents in the Christian family.

RECYLE

Too often we think of marriage preparation as something the pastor does in his study the month before the wedding. Such a view is inadequate and often disastrous. In our opinion, crash preparation for marriage carried out immediately before the wedding does little to reduce divorce statistics.

The pastor may say needed things, and the young couple may even listen to some of them. But training for a lifetime of marriage needs to begin twenty years before the knot is tied. Parents should start the recycling process during the earliest years of childhood. The project grows into serious commitment and systematic instruction as older teenagers begin to think of themselves as future parents. When Mom and Dad do their jobs properly, the formal counseling sessions offered by the pastor just before the wedding will merely confirm what those young people have learned long ago at home.

TEACH THEM WHAT CHRISTIAN MARRIAGE IS

In the first chapter we talked about what a newly married couple should do to create a family atmosphere for their yet unborn children. Now it's twenty years later, and those children are about to become parents.

While recognizing that our own husband-wife and parent-child relations have been the most dominant influence (modeling), we should also deliberately plan to teach our teens what they need to know about marriage (instruction). Three aspects seem to rise to the fore:

1. The purpose of Christian marriage
2. Biblical roles for family members and how to carry them out
3. What problems and joys to expect and how to cope with them

Some will say those things can't be taught; they must be experienced. Others will complain that telling young people too much before marriage will take away the joy of discovery.

But our problem surely has never been teaching our children too much! And the fact remains that marriage is still the most important social and spiritual dimension of life, yet it remains the one that thousands enter ill-equipped and poorly prepared.

SHOW THEM A BIBLICAL MODEL

Nick Thompson is a Christian young man who just recently passed his eighteenth birthday. On the surface he appears to be serious, spiritually-minded, and quite mature. But Nick himself knows he is a troubled boy. His family has always been closely connected to the church, and both parents have held offices. The pastor and most of the other members think of the Thompsons as the ideal family. But Nick knows the inside story.

Recently he has had reason to doubt Dad's love for Mom. There's no evidence of overt infidelity and even very little arguing. But the positive side of the ledger is empty. Nick never sees his dad openly express love to his mom either verbally or physically. He's trying hard to assume that it's there, but the atmosphere of sterility has given Nick a problem about showing affection to anyone else.

Not only that, since he has been old enough to discuss family matters with his parents, Nick has discovered that Mr. Thompson tries to "adjust" figures on his income tax return, asks friends downtown to "fix" an occasional parking ticket, and speaks critically and unkindly about other church members when they disagree with his views.

Nick and Dad had a major blow-up last week over drugs. Although he has no desire to smoke marijuana himself, Nick defended legalization just on principle. Dad almost choked on his cigarette while denouncing anyone who would use drugs in any form.

Nick's problem? A credibility gap. Should he design a lifestyle like the one his parents tell him about or like the one they live? In the crucial years immediately preceding his own marriage Nick is watching a negative demonstration of biblical roles, behavior, and ethics in his own home.

WARN THEM ABOUT THE PITFALLS

Expect in advance that such warning will often be equated with nagging. When you think about it, Jeremiah and Ezekiel were considered nags by those to whom they ministered. At least six mine fields await teens during dating and engagement years. Parents who care warn their kids about:

1. Masturbation
2. Emotional confusion in romantic relationships
3. Lust and evil thoughts
4. Premarital sex
5. Missing or not caring about God's will
6. Premature marriage

Each of those danger zones has an alternative on the positive and biblical side.

1. Masturbation is a selfish practice that begins with impure thoughts and ends in uncontrollable habits. God's answer is *His ownership of both mind and body* (1 Corinthians 6:9-20; Colossians 3:1-14).
2. The emotional confusion in boy-girl relationships can be countered with a casual, diversified dating life that sees Christians of the opposite sex as genuine friends and not

always potential partners for sex or marriage (Proverbs 18:24; John 15:15).

3. Lust and evil thoughts are sin. We dare not excuse them, nor can we afford to feed them with erotic magazines, movies, and books (1 Timothy 1:7; Philippians 4:8-9; 2 Timothy 2:22).

4. Premarital sex is sin because God has ordained that sexual relations are to be confined within marriage (1 Corinthians 7:1-5; Hebrews 13:4).

5. Missing God's will does not automatically produce a life of misery and unhappiness, but our teens need to know how to consider God's choice of a marriage partner (John 7:17; Romans 12:1-2).

6. Premature marriage militates against the high-level, careful planning God wants His children to give to marriage and family (Ephesians 5:15-33).

The local church should also assist parents in helping Christian teens prepare for marriage. Classes, youth programs, sex education, and counseling are supportive of what parents are doing in the home to show and tell what Christian marriage is all about.

LET GO!

Sometimes we talk about "the final years of parenting," but of course, parenting never ends. Somehow it just turns into grandparenting, and Christian adults in their fifties and sixties frequently find themselves engaged in both levels of leadership at the same time.

Donald Joy has written an interesting article entitled "The Seasons of a Family's Life," in which he develops the work of Daniel Levinson, Gail Sheehy, and Eric Ericson. The twenties he identifies as the decade of "pair bonding"—intimacy versus isolation. The thirties represent vocation and the developing of adult competence. The forties force a facing of reality with a "now or never" warning and the necessity of transferring the baton. Joy talks about the fifties as "the household in order" and indicates how productive those later years can be.[3]

But there are nagging questions plaguing Christian parents faced with launching the next generation. Consider these three more common ones.

WILL OUR CHILD HAVE FAITH?

That is a question John Westerhoff asked in an article some years ago. He wisely pointed out that "having faith" can mean a number of different things, and in the article he explores four different levels of faith, which may help us.

The first is the *experiential* level, which is essentially childhood faith. Remember your first church experience? I can recall sitting at the back of a Baptist church in a large eastern city. On Sunday evening the lights would dim and the illuminated cross at the front would signal the congregation's singing of the old hymn "Jesus Keep Me Near the Cross." That was a childhood faith experience of enormous significance even without the accompanying theological understanding it may have held for adults.

The second is the *affiliative* level, which Westerhoff claims describes adolescence beginning somewhere around the age of twelve. A strong sense of belonging and affirmation can emerge from a positive church experience during these years. When families fail to provide that kind of faith experience, teenagers often turn to cults and radical groups.

The third level is the *searching* level, and it hits right at the launch pad during late adolescence and young adulthood. How common it is to see a newly married Christian couple, inexplicably less interested in the things of the church than they were even as teenagers. Their new and autonomous family unit is reestablishing the whole faith format. Often their shaky attendance and sagging interest rebounds with great impact at the

3. Donald Joy, "The Seasons of a Family's Life," *Asbury Theological Seminary Herald*, Summer 1982, pp. 20-21.

birth of their first child. There they see the family faith community surfacing again.

But the highest and most important level is *ownership*. Here we're looking at constant reality in the application of spiritual values along with a commitment to absolutes and permanence. It is that kind of faith that we want to pass on to our next generation of families.

WILL HIS FAMILY BE HEALTHY?

We're not talking about freedom from measles, occasional allergies, and flu, but the overall sense of family wholeness. Dolores Curran has written a wonderful book entitled *Traits of a Healthy Family,* in which she exhibits fifteen items uncovered in her research that seem to characterize healthy families. Even though the book makes no Christian claims, almost every one of those items can be reinterpreted within the framework of biblical family living. According to Curran, the healthy family

1. communicates and listens
2. affirms and supports one another
3. teaches respect for others
4. develops a sense of trust
5. has a sense of play and humor
6. exhibits a sense of shared responsibility
7. teaches a sense of right and wrong
8. has a strong sense of family in which rituals and traditions abound
9. has a balance of interaction and sharing
10. has a shared religious core
11. respects the privacy of one another
12. values service to others
13. fosters table time and conversation
14. shares leisure time
15. admits to and seeks help with problems[4]

4. Dolores Curran, *Traits of a Healthy Family* (Minneapolis: Winston Press, 1983), pp. 23-24.

Quite a line-up, isn't it? But remember we don't start praying for our grown children and grandchildren to develop healthy families; we show them for twenty years precisely how a healthy family operates and then expect them to reproduce in kind!

WILL THE TORCH OF CHRISTIAN NURTURE BE PASSED?

Few serious Christian parents would consider that their children have faith or that their children's families are healthy unless succeeding generations pass on the godly heritage of the past. Nurture ties those three together. Somehow we must find balance between Christian education *in* the home (family nurture) and Christian education *of* the home (family life education). The former takes place in family rooms, bedrooms, kitchens, and backyards, whereas the latter takes place in auditoriums, classrooms, conferences, and camps.

Church and family join hands to take responsibility for the passing of the torch. But our position is that the major responsibility remains with the parents. The torch is passed when we have taught our children how to teach their children through both designed and undesigned teachable moments. Undesigned teachable moments are more frequent and generally more valuable—questions, events, traditions, special visitors in the home, crises, and anything that invokes opportunity to teach. Designed teachable moments fall into the category of normal instruction—family devotions, family games, mealtime discussions, bedtime stories, and prayer.

When our children were about four and seven we began traveling quite regularly during summers to Bible conferences and camps. That ministry continued every year, and our children traveled with us annually until they left for college.

During those years we visited almost every state and seventeen foreign countries. Our children were exposed to many excellent Bible teachers, camp counselors, missionary families, and other cultures and observed natural theology through much of God's magnificent creation.

Many teachable moments presented themselves as we played games in the station wagon, ate picnics at roadside parks, had devotions in a little rowboat, hiked the Alps, or admired the beauty of the west Canada coastline while landing in a small sea plane at a remote island camp.

When we have handed over a biblical, spiritual, and positive view of Christ, Scripture, church, and family, we have successfully launched the next generation, a task to which committed parents dedicate themselves for at least a quarter of a century.

Questions for Discussion

1. Could the loneliness described by the teenager who ran away ever happen in a Christian home? Under what circumstances? What would you do if faced with a similar situation?
2. How flexible can Christian parents be in recognizing the different values and interests of their teens?
3. What other issues would you list as causing conflict between Christian beliefs and those of the world? What are some biblical answers to those conflicts?
4. The chapter suggests that Christian parents should prepare teenagers for the problems and joys of marriage. What are some of those problems and joys?
5. What specific things can Christian parents do during the late teen years and even into the early twenties to prepare their children for marriage?

PART THREE

Problems and Issues
in Family Life

9

Discipline and Punishment

A sea of dirty faces, stringy hair, and wiggly bodies relayed its familiar signal to Sarah Long. This was, after all, her fifteenth year of teaching elementary schoolchildren, a challenge that still stirred excitement in her heart. She had to admit, however, that things were different now than in the mid-1970s when she had begun. Even in those days, after the rebellion of the sixties had quieted down some, most parents supported the programs, the teachers, and were reasonably available to help their children with homework and extracurricular activities. The intervening fifteen years had witnessed unprecedented family disintegration, which had begun to take an obvious toll on the smooth functioning of virtually any school classroom.

At long last American education is taking a hard look at itself and not liking what it sees. In virtually every urban school district, and increasingly in suburban districts, discipline surfaces as the number one problem of American public education. One survey carried out in Dade County, Florida (Miami), asked 9,700 teachers to name their dominant problems. First place went to the control or prevention of student misbehavior. No wonder. In that school system the number of school crimes (including everything from rape to vandalism) has risen to more than 10,000 a year.

Of course, school problems simply reflect the lack of discipline in the family. Having long ago abandoned absolute standards of ethics, morality, and behavior, the family stands in no position to solve the problem. We live in a permissive society in which rebellion, constantly on the increase, prepares the way for the ultimate lawless one, the Antichrist (2 Thessalonians 2:1-12).

Slowly we're learning that it's impossible to disassociate the Christian family from the society that surrounds it; our children and teenagers are affected by the permissive culture all around them. With regularity the culture tempts them to abandon parental standards and snub parental authority.

This national disease may be reaching epidemic proportions. One recent Gallup survey asked respondents to examine six options and answer the question, Which of these would you say is the main fault of parents in raising children nowadays? Here are the results:

> No discipline; parents too lenient; children have it too easy, 37%
> Children neglected, unattended, 8%
> Parents set poor example, 8%
> Children not treated as persons, given too little responsibility, 7%
> Lack of understanding, sympathy, 6%
> Children have too much money, 2%
> All others, 2%
> Don't know, 14%[1]

Obviously, we are dealing with a genuine problem here. How can we attack it?

---

1. "Neglect, Lack of Discipline Cited as Major Failures in Parenting," *Emerging Trends*, December 1984, p. 3.

A Biblical Model

Only two-thirds of Sarah's teaching tenure was spent in public schools; at the beginning of her eleventh year she switched to a teaching post at a Christian school—only to find many of the same problems—parents were frustrated and discouraged but seemed to genuinely want help. Experience and dedication had prepared Sarah to tackle problems head on. Singlehandedly she spearheaded a program to educate parents in child discipline. This veteran teacher understood that discipline problems among children were reflections of discipline problems in the lives of their parents.

In reality, unless we solve the problem of discipline and rebellion at the adult level, we will never solve it at the youth level. That forces us right back to the home, to the family context, and to the Word of God. Many passages in both Old and New Testaments deal with discipline, but few are more insightful than the twelfth chapter of the book of Hebrews. The immediate context deals with the Heavenly Father's spiritual nurture of His earthly children. But the comparison to earthly parenting is essential to the text, which contains at least seven disciplinary principles of great value to Christian parents.

DISCIPLINE IS A NECESSARY COMPONENT OF LOVE (vv. 5-6)

The Lord disciplines those whom He loves and punishes those He receives. Obviously parental discipline offered by Christians within the family context should always be loving—never administered in anger. No emotional outburst of irrationality, a loving response points out the wrong, explains the reason for punishment, and proceeds with forgiveness.

DISCIPLINE AND PUNISHMENT ARE NOT THE SAME (v. 6)

Two different words are used in verse 6 to identify discipline and punishment; we shall treat that more thoroughly in just a moment.

DISCIPLINE IDENTIFIES THE CHILD AS A BONA-FIDE MEMBER OF HIS FAMILY (vv. 7-8)

The reference to earthly fathers in these verses indicates again that God teaches us spiritual truth through physical and particularly family illustrations. How do we know we belong to the family of God? One indication is that He disciplines us to bring us into line when we displease Him. Uncontrolled, undisciplined children might as well not be in a family. And as we have noted earlier, even teenagers subconsciously feel a genuine need for control and discipline, though they may outwardly flaunt permissiveness.

DISCIPLINE BY HUMAN PARENTS IS NEVER PERFECT (vv. 9-10)

Scripture teaches that we are to reverence, or honor, parents who correct us, even when they do it imperfectly and sometimes at their own whim. Discipline must be accepted, indeed welcomed, by Christian children and teenagers because parents hold their authoritative positions by divine appointment. And, since we all know our discipline and punishment techniques are faulty, it may help from time to time to tell our children just that.

DISCIPLINE ALWAYS SEEMS PAINFUL AT THE TIME, BUT PRODUCES FRUIT IN THE END (v. 11)

When the task gets discouraging, Christian parents must remember the reward. We know we're attempting to do God's will, yet sometimes our efforts at discipline and punishment seem to stir up greater rebellion and achieve negative results. Successful disciplining requires patience, persistence, and keeping the end in view.

DISCIPLINE REQUIRES COURAGE ON THE PART OF CHRISTIAN PARENTS
(vv. 12-13)

Are your hands tired? Knees feeble? Feet a little shaky? God says don't be discouraged, don't give up. Rebellion is sin, and it must be dealt with.

DISCIPLINE AND PUNISHMENT, PROPERLY APPLIED, WILL LEAD TO
HOLINESS (v. 14)

Peace? Holiness? In our family? It seems like an elusive dream, but it is clearly one of the results of a proper approach to discipline in the Christian home—God has promised it.

A Significant Difference

The difference between discipline and punishment is unclear in the minds of many parents. Punishment is used when discipline fails. Discipline erects fences; punishment comes when a child breaks the fences down or deliberately transgresses the boundaries. Parents incorrectly conclude that a slap in the face is discipline. It is not. It is punishment, and probably a poor form of it.

DISCIPLINE PRECEDES PUNISHMENT

A parent who administers punishment before the boundaries, rules, and "fences" of discipline have been established is engaging in unjust and unproductive behavior. Nurture, not negation; cultivation, not confinement, is the primary concern. We like the way William Payne describes the issue.

> The purpose of discipline is to help a child learn to behave in a desirable, safe way and to respect the property and feelings of others. It is to direct him toward what he *can* do, where he can ride his bike, dig holes, and pound pots and pans, rather than where he *can't*. The Commandments provide a pattern, and you can "talk" about them when you are at home or out

at home or out for a walk; at bedtime and the first thing in the morning (Deuteronomy 6:7; 11:19).[2]

DISCIPLINE PRESUPPOSES PUNISHMENT

Only people who believe in original sin can understand this principle. Advocates of good or neutral natures in children argue that they should never need punishment at all, assuming the environment is correct. The Bible teaches that the environment is only one part of the complex; the evil sin nature in every child's heart is even more important. Punishment will at times be necessary. It flows out of discipline. In the same way, the presentation of the Mosaic law revealed the disobedience of the children brought forth the necessity of punishment. The law didn't cause disobedience, but it did reveal it.

The parable of the prodigal son in Luke 15 implies that rebellion is actually a form of mental unbalance. Verse 17 of that chapter tells us the young man finally "came to his senses." The Greek word implies that he finally got his mind straightened out or, in contemporary jargon, got his head together. His rebellion was a form of irrationality, and the behavior of his father in handling it demonstrates love, patience, grace, and willingness to forgive.

Nevertheless, the overall picture of Scripture demands that Christian parents lead their children and teenagers from the basic sinful, natural state of rebellion to a place of enforced discipline, which can then lead to self-discipline and ultimately to Christ-discipline as they surrender their lives to His lordship. Ancient wisdom works today: "Correct your son, and he will give you comfort; he will also delight your soul" (Proverbs 29:17, NASB*).

Remember Sarah Long's elementary school children? She made a commitment to working with the students' parents. Of course, not every parent responded to her program, but, among

New American Standard Bible.
2. William G. Payne, Jr., "Discipline and Punishment—Where Do You Stand?" *Parent Talk* 1, no. 7 (n.d.), p. 1.

the children of those who did, a gradual but distinct transformation began to take place. They learned to function within the bounds of behavior, slowly backing away from the need to constantly press authority to the widest possible limit. The commitment of their families made the difference.

DISCIPLINE PREPARES FOR PUNISHMENT

When telling our children what they can and cannot do we must also tell them what will happen when they violate family rules. Disciplined parents tend to produce disciplined children by the very nature of the order and spirit in the home. Paul Kienel reminds us:

> Good discipline begins with instruction. Without it you can expect a severe case of rebellion in the heart of your children. Make it clear to your youngsters what you expect of them. Discipline without instruction is unscriptural and unfair. "And, ye fathers provoke not your children to wrath; but bring them up in the nurture (discipline) and admonition (instruction) of the Lord." Biblical discipline requires a balance of instruction with discipline.[3]

A PARENTAL IMPERATIVE

There was a time in American life when social values and spiritual values overlapped—but that time has passed. Today's neo-secular society forces tremendous tension on teenagers to conform to the relative norms of their culture, a culture influenced by the deteriorating standards of adult behavior. The generation we are rearing now as children and young people has inherited the affluent materialism of contemporary America along with the myth that we have somehow achieved this by our own hard work or our own innate goodness. Christian parents committed to biblical ideals will de-emphasize the fable of civil religion and morality and concentrate on God's grace and

3. Paul A. Kienel, "Seven Keys to Family Discipline," *Christian School Comment* 8, no. 5 (n.d.), p. 1.

biblical mandates for behavior. It is not an option; it is an imperative.

ERECT FENCES WISELY

Think again of discipline as a fence. If the fences are too close to the house, the child has insufficient room to play, appears constantly frustrated, and is therefore often punished. If the fences are too far from the house, the child could get into trouble, get lost, or wander where parents can't observe his behavior, and punishment almost never takes place, however often it should have occurred.

When the fences are carefully planned and erected in just the right places, discipline and punishment can stay in balance. And remember that the during the process of growth from dependence to independence, the boundaries must be gradually widened. Notice that the fence principle operates in the simple command illustrated in the diagram on page 123.

AIM FOR THE HIGHEST KIND OF DISCIPLINE

There are three kinds of discipline—enforced discipline, self-discipline, and Christ-discipline. Unfortunately, we too often emphasize the first and forget that the entire process of nurture and growth leads children and young people to the second and then ultimately to the third.

It may be simplistic, but we could say that young children are greatly in need of *enforced discipline*; teenagers ought to be well on their way to exercising wise *self-discipline*; and adults ought to be functioning under voluntary *Christ-discipline*, living their lives in accordance with the instruction of the Holy Spirit through Scripture (encapsuled in Paul's words in Romans 6:9-18).

BE PROMPT, BE FAIR, BE UNITED

Promptness in punishment does not necessarily mean striking a child immediately as he pulls up all the flowers you

"Do Your Homework Right After School"

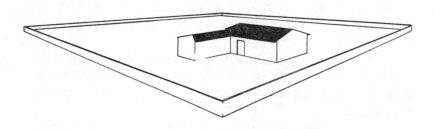

"Do Your Homework"

"Do Your Homework Before Watching Television"

just planted. It does mean administering the reward of his deeds while the behavior is still well in mind. The time delay can be extended with older children and teens, but with young children instant linkage is crucial.

Fairness is not as obvious as it might first appear. Sometimes parents engage in what has politely been called "entrapment" rather than giving their children the benefit of the doubt until they prove they can't be trusted. And remember that no single set of rules or punishment fits every child, although the levels of discipline and punishment among several children in the family must be kept in balance.

Unite the efforts of husband and wife in the two-parent family. Somewhere we've got the idea that nurture belongs to the mother and punishment is the task of the father. That conclusion is impractical, unbiblical, and dangerous. Parents should agree on family rules, communicate the rules as a team, and share in all necessary punishment or other kinds of back-up support.

Our two children were very different in their temperaments. Parents with three, four, or more say it doesn't matter how many children you have, each one develops into a unique personality.

Our son, Jeff, was sensitive and easily corrected. Because of his tender spirit, a cross word or stern look would often correct his improper behavior. When the house was quiet we could probably find him sitting on the floor surrounded by toys or a book.

Julie was another case altogether. During her preschool years, a quiet house told us we had better check on her whereabouts. She was often found eating the dirt from a flower pot or pulling all the toilet paper off the roll and making a pretty pile on the floor. Our approach to correction with her required greater firmness and regularity.

The writer of Hebrews ends the passage discussed earlier with "See that no one is sexually immoral, or is godless like Esau, who for a single meal sold his inheritance rights as the oldest son" (Hebrews 12:16). Perhaps God is warning Christian parents not to "raise an Esau," whose worldly behavior and lack of concern for spiritual values was characterized most dramatically by undisciplined behavior.

Questions for Discussion

1. Do you believe the authors' distinction between discipline and punishment is correct? How would you modify it?
2. What specific ways can Christian parents develop orderly disciplined patterns with young children? With young teens? With older teens?
3. Do you believe in physical punishment? What forms are most helpful? How do you handle the various biblical texts (notably Proverbs) that seem to affirm the value of physical punishment?
4. Why is it important for husband and wife to present a united front in dealing with the matters of discipline and punishment? How can they best do that?
5. What trends or issues do you foresee in the next ten years that will make the issue of discipline and punishment either less important or more important for Christian parents?

10

Family Worship

Bill and Sue Langley are determined to be effective Christian parents. Each day they gather their three children around the table after supper for a half hour of family worship. Together they read the Bible, pray, and join in an occasional song.

Sounds good, doesn't it? But all is not well at Langley family worship. Greg (fifteen) resents missing his favorite television program. Cindy (twelve) complains that she can't spare the time from homework responsibilities. Steve (seven) shows his disinterest by making noises and disturbing the others. The more the children fuss, the more Bill and Sue force the issue. Some evenings family worship erupts into a verbal battle upsetting everyone for the next several hours.

Where have the Langleys gone wrong? Rather than answering that question directly, let us take a look at some of the issues involved in effective family worship. Then perhaps the problems at the Langley house will become more obvious, and we can pinpoint helpful solutions.

BIBLICAL FOUNDATIONS

Some people think the Bible contains many passages on the importance and technique of family worship. Actually it does not. But the general tone of both Old and New Testaments certainly presents the theme—the home is the central source of spiritual teaching in God's plan. Listen to Moses' words recorded in Deuteronomy 6:4-9:

> O Israel, listen: Jehovah is our God, Jehovah alone. You must love him with all your heart, soul, and might. And you must think constantly about these commandments I am giving you today. You must teach them to your children and talk about them when you are at home or out for a walk; at bedtime and the first thing in the morning. Tie them on your finger, wear them on your forehead, and write them on the doorposts of your house! (TLB)

OLD TESTAMENT PRACTICES

Imagine the splendor of Adam's walk with God in the Garden of Eden. That was true worship! All the early books of the Old Testament emphasize the worship of God, and before Genesis ends we find that worship centered in family relationships (Genesis 49:8).

Passover was the greatest worship experience for Jewish families, and in the law respect for the Sabbath became major family duty (Exodus 20:10). There was a strong negative message too—any kind of idolatrous worship would unleash the wrath of God (Deuteronomy 8:19).

The Old Testament also closely links worship with service. God's people of ancient times served first within the family itself, then among other families, spreading out to the tribal groups and ultimately to the world. A godly family during the days of Moses learned to relate in a serving way to four groups of people: "And the Levite, because he has no portion or inheritance among you, and the alien, the orphan, and the widow who are in your town, shall come and eat and be satisfied, in order that the Lord your God may bless you and all the work of your hand which you do" (Deuteronomy 14:29).

As late as the time of the prophet Joel we see national worship centering in the family.

Blow the trumpet in Zion, declare a holy fast, call a sacred assembly. Gather the people, consecrate the assembly; bring together the elders, gather the children, those nursing at the breast. Let the bridegroom leave his room and the bride her chamber. (Joel 2:15-16)

In the later history of the nation, Jewish leaders began to follow such commands by literally tying boxes to their foreheads and left arms. The small containers, called phylacteries, held tiny scrolls with four passages from the Old Testament. That kind of rigid legalism called forth Jesus' condemnation of the Pharisees.

Surely the passage is meant to be symbolic. Moses might have said, "The things of the Lord should fill your homes at all times. Be free to talk about spiritual matters with your children just as normally as you would discuss anything else."

We stand in danger of making the same mistake when we engage in ritualistic family worship. Spiritual times with our children should never resemble the sterile practice of "tying boxes on foreheads and wrists."

NEW TESTAMENT PRACTICES

From the earliest pages of the New Testament, we learn of the importance of worship and how it requires family involvement. People seemed to sense the significance of bringing little children into contact with Jesus, and His love for them was obvious (Luke 18:15-17).

For children, worship usually occurs spontaneously in a moment of awe and awareness of God. We remember the day our dog Spooky gave birth to seven squirming balls of fur. Sitting around the well prepared birthing area, our family watched in amazement as God brought forth life from one of his creatures. Our children talked about how God had prepared her to know just what to do with those pups. As she cleaned and protected each one, we sat in silent worship of the Almighty Creator who had planned even the smallest details in His world.

Family faith sustained the New Testament church, which placed great emphasis on home relationships. The early church met in homes where young children were exposed continuously to an atmosphere of worship and praise to Jesus.

The apostle Paul makes plain in his writings to Titus and Timothy that worship in public without prior worship in the family perverts God's plan. The same holds true in service. Anyone who would seek a position of leadership in the public assembly must first learn to lead at home (1 Timothy 3:1-7).

GENERAL PRINCIPLES

In his section on family devotions in the very helpful encyclopedic volume *Parents & Teenagers*, Larry Richards sorts out the difference between an Old Testament and New Testament approach to family devotions. The New Testament concept, he observes, centers on the priesthood of all believers. Based on that principle he "decided to change our family experience to a two-way communication pattern, so that everyone was functioning as a believer/priest rather than a recipient of my word as lord."[1]

It may be important to note that the Bible does not dictate procedures for family worship. The Father allows each Christian family to define for itself how the practice of devotions can best be exercised in their home. We like the idea of a universal priesthood approach and suggest the following principles which many Christian parents have found helpful.

FLEXIBILITY

Try to avoid strict authoritarianism in such matters as time, format, and style of family worship. Mottos like "No Bible-No Breakfast" are catchy and may have some value in self-discipline, but severe restrictions probably hinder rather than help

---

1. Larry Richards, "Family Devotions—To Have Them or Not?" in *Parents & Teens*, Jay Kesler, ed. (Wheaton, Ill.: Victor, 1984) p. 345.

achieve productivity in family life. Many families find that the morning rush just will just not tolerate additional activities.

Implementation has to be flexible too. Barry St. Clair reminds us to "apply what you discuss to everyday life. After each meeting, ask, 'what can you do today to practice what we just learned?' Then the next time you meet, follow up by asking, 'how did your plan work out?'"[2]

Be careful about legalism here. Don't feel guilty when you miss a day; don't allow the children to believe that God will somehow love them less or protect them carelessly if family devotions has somehow been neglected. Nobody can determine your best time for family worship—you'll have to find that out through prayer and open discussion with all family members.

PRACTICALITY

Family worship should be fitted to the children's interests and needs. High level discussions of theological issues are good for husbands and wives but can be deadly at family devotions. The more children and teens talk during family worship, the more parents can understand their problems and show ways that God's Word addresses those problems. When the rest of the family sits and listens to Dad preach, practicality drops to a low ebb.

One family in our church uses family devotions to review the Bible stories their children heard in Sunday school the previous week. With the tape recorder running, the children tell the stories in their own words then, amid laughter and occasional embarrassment, the whole family listens as the story is played back. The idea is a good one for several reasons. First, it gives the parents a chance to discuss with their children some of the things they have been learning. Second, the child becomes a participant, not just an observer during family worship. Finally,

2. Barry St. Clair, "Steps to Starting a Family Worship Time," *Parents & Teens*, p. 348.

parents can be sure that children will not be bored when recording or listening to themselves on tape.

Let's not be guilty of going through the motions of worship just for the sake of doing it. It may relieve our guilt, but it does not produce true family worship.

NATURALNESS

As Deuteronomy 6 implies, don't make family worship into anything extraordinary. It should be a usual and expected pattern in the home. Too much fanfare gives it the appearance of being something abnormal rather than a common part of Christian family life. Every time Bill Langley forces the issue, he may be building resistance in his teenagers.

We have found that naturalness links up nicely with flexibility and practicality in family worship. Sometimes when on vacation we have stopped for a picnic lunch and taken time for Bible reading and prayer by a brook or under a tree. We can recall evenings when it was just too pleasant outside to stay inside around the table for our family worship. Common sense called for immediate adjournment to the patio or backyard for devotions under the stars. Teachable moments are not created by trenchant rigidity but by the natural experience of life. Like learning, worship comes to us in that kind of context.

PRACTICAL GUIDELINES

Most Christian parents vote in favor of family worship. Their constant questions focus more on the how than the why. But patterns that have worked for some families may not be helpful for others. Some general guidelines may be useful. What do you think of these?

VARIATION

G. Weatherly writes, "Interest will be retained as parents keep their family devotions from becoming a meaningless routine of doing the same thing in the same way at the same time each day. Planned variety can prevent this from happening."[3] We agree. Attention spans of small children require multiple and differing activities, and adults like variety too.

Sometimes family worship may include only singing, discussing a troubling situation, reading some good Christian fiction (like *The Chronicles of Narnia*, by C. S. Lewis), or just taking a walk to enjoy a sunset. The important thing is that children's faith be strengthened in an unusual way when they see God answer specific needs for which they have prayed rather specifically and perhaps repeatedly in family worship.

PARTICIPATION

Family worship should not be a time when dad plays pastor. Most children enjoy getting into the act and will enthusiastically do what they are asked. Devotions then involve the total family. At one point when our children were growing up we concluded that we could only have family devotions four nights a week. Sunday and Wednesday we spent at church and Saturday night we were often involved in some fun activity and were often away from home.

With four members in our family it seemed logical to put one person in charge of each night—and it worked. Our young son once conceived the idea of having family devotions around a campfire in the back yard, and, when still a preschooler, our daughter once asked Dad to read Acts 12, then retold the story five-year-old style and took a closing offering! (We think all the money went into the Sunday school offering the next week.)

Remember that true participation includes delegation, so worship leaders should be free to plan any kind of program they want. Parents may need to offer suggestions, and a few reminders may be in order to encourage proper planning. Such a system might not work indefinitely (we found it effective for about two years). Be creative, have fun, and don't get tense.

3. G. Weatherly, "Family Devotions That Thrill," *Sunday School Times and Gospel Herald*, December 1, 1972, p. 22.

HABITUATION

Like individuals, families get into habits. Sometimes the habits are not helpful—like missing church whenever you have Sunday company. But family worship should become a habit that draws family members together and makes each one feel he or she is contributing to, as well as drawing on, the family's spiritual resources.

David Veerman reminds us that consistency is crucial.

> Too often the attempts are intense and sporadic. Dad will insist on devotions everyday at dinner time; but because of schedule conflicts and interruptions, this effort lasts about a week. Instead, we should decide in advance which days (and time of day) are best suited. Then we must follow through with few exceptions and insist that everyone is present. Consistency will produce expectancy and habit, and will reinforce the importance of the study.[4]

COMMON ERRORS

Family worship usually turns sour when we fall into one or more of the following traps. Check each one in conjunction with Bill Langley's problems—and, perhaps, your own.

1. Beginning too late—family worship should be a life-style for children from the earliest possible age.
2. Inadequate materials—adult devotional booklets and difficult Bible translations don't help the cause.
3. Forced involvement—pressure to conform is not always good, especially with teenagers.
4. Rigid adherence—don't let guilt clouds hang over the family when devotions are missed once in a while.

---

4. David Veerman, "Dusting Off the Family Altar," *Parents & Teens*, p. 348.

5. Carelessness—lack of planning, frequent forgetting, and irrelevance all tend to deteriorate the importance of family worship.

The main thing is to start where you are now. Put behind you the failures of the past. Explain to your children and teens why family patterns need to change, how they can be changed, and humbly ask for their cooperation. God's grace can indeed cover a multitude of sins and blunders.

Questions for Discussion

1. Is prayer before meals a form of family worship? Can it be? Should it be?
2. How soon are young children able to participate in family worship? What can we do about their short attention spans?
3. Name some ways in which children of various ages can be involved in family worship.
4. If a family has not conducted group devotions until the children are teenagers, how can they successfully start at that point?
5. List at least ten different activities that could be part of effective family worship.

11

Choosing a School—Public, Private, or Home

This year almost 50 million children and teenagers will attend America's schools. Thousands of American families will arrange their schedules around football practice, play rehearsal, cheerleading tryouts, and other activities. We are a nation of schoolgoers, convinced that chalkboards and desks are natural parts of life.[1]

Furthermore, an overwhelming percentage of your child's time is spent in school or school-related activities (approximately 40-50 percent of his waking hours during the weeks when school is in session).

Christian parents face a genuine dilemma on this question. How can believers respond to a pagan state that requires education but also refuses to take responsibility for inculcation of spiritual and moral values? To put it even more simply, where should your child go to school? And why? Perhaps your family is facing the same decision currently troubling the Nel-

---

1. Much of the material in this chapter has been adapted from an article entitled "The Educated Choice," which appeared in *Kindred Spirit*, Fall 1984. Additional information on Christian schools appears in chapters 43 and 44 of *Church Education Handbook*, published by Victor Books in 1985.

sons. Matt Nelson, an electrical engineer, spent all his educational years in public school and at a community college. His wife, Connie, went to a high quality private high school and then into nurses' training in a hospital affiliated with the Roman Catholic church. Amy is five and ready to start kindergarten; little Josh, toddling along behind, has just passed his second birthday.

Living in a suburb of a large city offers several possibilities for the Nelsons. Public schools in the area have an excellent academic reputation, and most of the neighbors are delighted to be living in such a good school district. But Connie understands that their evaluation stems not from biblical values but from a normal and expected worldly perspective. What are her options?

The Case for Public Schools

Those who recommend public schools for Christian children may remind us that the early Christians availed themselves of the Roman public school system, blatantly pagan as it was. They did so because there was no other choice, a reality that faces many sincere Christian parents in our day. However, the early Christians entertained no wild-eyed notions of reforming the public school system nor did they minimize the reality of the satanic atmosphere in which their children had to live in order to obtain an education.

PROBLEMS IN THE PUBLIC SCHOOL

To be sure, the blatant use of drugs and exposure to constant immorality does not permeate every public school in America, but it certainly does characterize most large urban systems and increasingly forms the standard in suburban systems as well. "But," you say, "in our town there is still a strong sense of morality, and many public school teachers are Christians." Great! But don't assume then that your local school sets the standard for American education in the 1980s. More likely it represents a rare exception.

SUPPORT FOR THE PUBLIC SCHOOL

Thinking Christians should not oppose all public education. For the unbeliever in a secular society, the American system of education may rate as the finest in the history of the world. But Christian children are citizens of a different "country," with a different set of values and standards, and a very different idea of truth. As professional educators, we believe that the children of God deserve something better than pagan public education. When we give our sons and daughters to the secular system we invite the values, standards, and errors of a godless culture to penetrate their spirits. And God had made parents responsible for those spirits (Deuteronomy 6:20-23).

Many today, both inside and outside the public school, believe that the system will eventually self-destruct. Continuing conflict over bussing and quota systems, teacher strikes in major cities almost every fall, the liberal lobby of the National Education Association, and consistently falling SAT scores match up with an uncontrollable drug problem and mounting violence. Each month 282,000 students and 5,200 teachers are assaulted in public schools. Twenty-five percent of all schools experience some violence monthly.

MINISTRY IN THE PUBLIC SCHOOL

Despite its problems, however, the public school presents a place of important ministry for many Christians. For some urban school teachers the primary task is survival not communication. But there are many school opportunities in which the holy presence of a servant of the Lord can demonstrate His love and melt hardened hearts.

Among the early Christians a book called *The Canons of Hyppolytus* affirmed that a Christian teacher might teach in a public school if he clearly announced his belief in Jesus Christ, denied all pagan deities, and used his post as an opportunity for evangelism. That kind of witness is tough in modern America, but some godly teachers still find ways to make it work.

May their service be blessed of God. Ron Allen reminds us to consider the Old Testament patterns before we abandon the public school system.

> Before you change schools, consider all the issues. Young Jewish boys faced problems in Nebuchadnezzar's court in the sixth century B.C. Those very problems, which were at least as awful as those that may face your children, became opportunities for God to triumph in the lives of Daniel, Hananiah, Mishael and Azariah. The parents of these young men had no choice in the matter of their "schooling." We, however, have choices to make. By God's grace we may believe He is able to work for good even in a difficult situation.[2]

THE CASE FOR CHRISTIAN SCHOOLS

Are Christian schools still popular in the late 1980s? They surely are, and gaining in numbers every day. Just one group, the Association of Christian Schools, International, claims 364,070 students in 2,148 schools in the United States. That represents phenomenal growth in the past decade and can clearly be identified as a trend in the last quarter of the twentieth century. Some claim that as many as 20,000 Christian schools enroll more than 2 million students in America today.

As a result of their ongoing exploration regarding Amy's schooling, Matt and Connie Nelson have discovered a large Baptist church less than five miles from their home. The elementary school operated by the church (K-8) uses an excellent curriculum, and the teachers demand strict behavioral standards. In some ways the school reminds Connie of her rather conservative Catholic school, though, of course, the doctrinal differences are immediately obvious. She feels comfortable with the thought of Amy's going to the Baptist school, but Matt claims it's just another unnecessary expense, especially at the lower elementary level. How will they make their decision?

2. Ronald B. Allen, "A Case for Public Schools," *Moody Monthly*, March 1986, p. 14.

PROPER MOTIVATION

Why do parents send their children to Christian schools? Sometimes for the wrong reasons—racism, absence of prayer in the public schools, or an attempt to get special handling of disciplinary problems. Others really want an atmosphere of morality or serious academics.

The real reasons for enrolling children in Christian schools center in the foundations for truth and the opportunity for parental voice. But, as Pilate once asked, what is truth? Public education deals in *relative* truth, ideas constantly in a state of flux. "Truth" today might not be "truth" tomorrow.

The Word of God is *absolute* truth. The God of the Bible never changes. His truth does not vary from one day to the next, nor does it become outdated and in need of constant reworking. Christian education emphasizes absolute truth based on eternal values. The two systems stand in genuine disharmony; the issue of God's revelation divides Christians and non-Christians right at the beginning of educational discussions (2 Timothy 3:14-17).

But parental voice is important, too, and there's not much of that left in the public school system. "Family life education" in secular schools has little to do with obedience and respect for parents. It focuses rather on the appropriate use of contraceptives for premarital sex and the acceptance of homosexuality as an alternative life-style—a sad substitute for what teens need.

QUALITY CONTROL

In affirming the validity of the Christian school, several concerns need be voiced. One is the matter of *quality control*. How can parents measure excellence in Christian education? Certainly three yardsticks must be applied—qualification, certification, and accreditation. *Qualification* deals with academic *and* theological dimensions. In our judgment, a Christian schoolteacher qualifies for that post only when both types of preparation are adequate.

Certification has to do with meeting the educational establishment where it is, and winning. Christian schools need to open themselves to proper inspection by legitimate examining bodies. Nothing can be gained by condemning state departments of education and retreating into self-righteous isolation. If you're considering a Christian school, please look for schools that make conscientious efforts to affirm their teachers' quality through certification.

Accreditation for elementary and secondary schools operates on two levels—regional and national. Secular associations have rigid requirements for member schools, and Christian schools often find it difficult to attain their standards—but many do. Private associations like ACSI and CSI measure doctrinal as well as educational qualities, and *all* schools should subject themselves to such examinations.

PAROCHIAL PARALYSIS

A second concern when considering the Christian school may be called *parochial paralysis.* Twenty years ago most Christian schools were parent-controlled societies in which duly elected board members carried on the decision-making, policy-setting process of the school. Though many schools still operate that way, new schools begun in the seventies and eighties have found such independence too expensive, especially when they can use the educational plants in large churches.

Today the popular parochial (church-controlled) model dominates the Christian school. Perhaps the pastor or some other member of the staff may also serve as the educational leader of the school. Such schools often expect or require teachers to join the sponsoring church (whose members may receive a tuition discount). Occasionally Christian schools flaunt their independence in the face of the law and refuse any outside standards for their educational programs. Such an attitude is not necessary, of course; church-controlled schools can and should provide high quality education.

PARENTAL PRIORITY

A third concern is the matter of *priority*. Since the home is God's primary institution, the Christian school may become its partner in building families, not test scores or top athletic teams. Christian parents want to hear less about the superiority of Christian schools over public schools and more about how those schools are gearing up to strengthen the moral and spiritual character of their students. What can Christian education do to strengthen the home? Provide family seminars? A special marriage and family course for seniors? Yes—those and other evidences of commitment to serving the home.

THE CASE FOR HOME SCHOOLS

Having exploded into the late twentieth century without warning, the home schooling movement is so new that statistics are still unreliable. We cannot calculate the number of children being taught by parents at home, but 250,000 may be a justifiable guess. As the idea gathers steam, home schooling may well establish itself as a trend. By 1990—or even earlier—the movement may be as significant a force in Christian education as Christian schools have been in the seventies and eighties.

Many court calendars now register suits and countersuits to establish whether parents have the right to teach their children at home. At the moment, the states make the decisions, but that policy may not always remain. Parents interested in home schools need to carefully investigate the legal boundaries in their states and find out how state statutes are interpreted at the local level.

ARE HOME SCHOOLS BIBLICAL?

William Barclay in his classic history of education, *Educational Ideals in the Ancient World,* explains that Old Testament education possessed two dominant traits: it was *theological,* and it was conducted in the *family* context. The formal classroom setting is a recent innovation compared to instruction under parental guidance. Remember that the three basic types of childhood learning (experience, modeling, and instruction—in that order) function much more naturally and extensively in the family context than in the contrived and plastic environment of an organized classroom. Daily repetition of godly habit patterns can fulfill Isaiah's call for consistency: "Who is it he is trying to teach? To whom is he explaining his message? To children weaned from their milk, to those just taken from the breast? For it is: do and do, do and do, rule on rule, rule on rule; a little here, a little there" (Isaiah 28:9-10).

ARE HOME SCHOOLS FOR EVERYONE?

Home schooling is definitely not for everyone. Cautions regarding home schools are every bit as important as the recognition of their validity. In spite of repeated reports of *socialization* studies, for example, years spent with siblings and parents (usually one parent in the teaching framework) probably do not compare with the peer socialization gained in larger groups of students called "classes." *Evaluation*, too, deserves our careful attention. Parents conducting home schooling experiences must regularly and systematically submit their children to authoritative testing procedures. That kind of objective analysis of their learning accomplishments is essential.

Is home schooling a good choice for Matt and Connie? Well, in the first place we're not talking about Matt *and* Connie. Matt's job requires eight to ten hours a day, so if any home schooling goes on Connie will have to do it. As a registered nurse she is certainly an educated person though hardly a specialist in early elementary education. She hasn't worked full-time since Amy was born, but she has kept in touch with her nursing skills by putting in two days a week at a doctor's office while the children go to a day care center. Insecure about her teaching capabilities, Connie has some genuine doubts about giving up her job and losing contact with the medical field altogether. And could she actually teach Amy with two year-old Josh to watch as well?

Much of the literature of the home school movement seems to suggest that home schooling can be carried out by almost any parent. But the *capability* of parents poses a major problem to home schooling. It involves more than just intellectual skills (although 23 million adults in America are functionally illiterate); parents must also be emotionally and socially ready to handle the task of maintaining an efficient school.

SHOULD WE HOME SCHOOL OUR CHILDREN?

Only husband and wife in consultation before the Lord can answer the question of whether to practice home schooling. The spiritual qualities of parents will determine whether the home school is distinctly Christian or not. We find it ironic that churches, parachurch organizations, and public schools have long complained that they have to take up the slack with children and teenagers because parents simply do not get the job done at home.

Would an effort at full-time home schooling for those children for several years solve the problem, or would parents whose inadequacies created the problems just complicate them by spending more time with the children? To be sure, these are pragmatic and not necessarily biblical questions, but they are important. The responsibility for home schooling demands much more than the promotional literature of the home school movement admits.

Home schools and Christian schools at all levels may be God's alternatives to pagan education in the late twentieth century. Parents need not be locked into the public schooling mentality of most Americans. Rather than concentrating undue concern on prayer amendments and reforming the public system, Christian educators should design creative alternatives that are genuinely Christian. The future is uncertain, especially if anarchy gives way to totalitarianism in America, as some suggest it may. But for the moment, parents can choose freedom instead of fear and parental rather than public control. Christians should exercise their options to the glory of God and the spiritual nurture of their children (Philippians 2:14-16).

Questions for Discussion

1. Do you believe it is specifically right or wrong for Christian parents to send their children to public schools? Defend your answer.
2. What are some of the wrong reasons for sending children to a Christian school?
3. What do you know about existing laws governing home schooling in your area?
4. Do you know any friends who are home schooling? How do you estimate their success?
5. Should Christians be involved in the founding of new Christian schools? Why? Why not?

12

Playing Together and Staying Together

Phil and Tammy Walters have a problem. They both work, and, as a two-income family, they have plenty of money. That's not the problem. Their generous companies provide satisfactory benefits including three weeks' vacation a year for Phil and two weeks for Tammy, so there is plenty of time to get away. That's not the problem either. But somehow, in the twisted thinking of their relationship they have decided that "vacation" means being away *from* rather than being away *with* the family. That fits in with their regular practice of "her night out" and "his night out" each week (they rarely go out together).

This is not a chapter on how to take vacations, but on how to keep the marriage and family together by using "discretionary time" for recreation. Nor will we get back into family devotions again, although there is something to be said for a balance between *playing* together and *praying* together as a means toward *staying* together, so we'll want to say something about that as well.

Divorce statistics defy explanation and change constantly, but the *Kiplinger Washington Letter* noted early in 1986 that there will be fewer first marriages in the years just ahead but more remarriages. In fact the latter will account for one-third of all marriages. Divorces, they tell us, zoomed in the seventies, dropped slightly around 1982-83, but have started up again. Some experts think half of all baby boom marriages will end up on the rocks, and most people who work with divorce statistics now talk about a 50 percent mortality rate.

In some major cities divorce rates are considerably higher (60 to 65 percent).[1] In 1985, for example, in Dallas County, Texas, 21,470 marriage licenses were granted compared to 22,933 in 1984. The number of divorces the same year, however, was 13,314 (1985) compared to 13,412 the year before. One could argue that as marriage rates drop, divorce rates also drop. But the key statistic is the relationship of divorces to marriages—62 percent! The National Center for Health Statistics reported a 49 percent divorce rate in 1985.[2] (Key Scripture passages dealing with divorce include Deuteronomy 24:1-4; Malachi 2:14-16; Matthew 5:31, 32; Matthew 19:3-10; Romans 7:1-3; 1 Corinthians 7:10-16.)

PLAYING TOGETHER

A recent newspaper headline blared the warning: "Family Disaster Feared." The writer quoted psychiatrist Graham G. Blaine, Jr., of the Harvard Medical Services, who suggests that alienation between children and their parents grows yearly. Neurotic illness, serious drug abuse, and delinquency also appear to be related to faulty family relationships. He proposes to restructure family life so that from babyhood through age seventeen, a child would be placed in the care of others from eight in the morning till six in the evening, six days a week, eleven months of the year!

Perhaps you react by saying, "The suggestion is ridiculous; parents will never agree to do such a thing." But many parents closely approach Blaine's idea even now. They become so ob-

1. *The Kiplinger Washington Letter*, February 14, 1986, p. 1.
2. "Marriages Decrease, Divorces Increase," *The Dallas Morning News*, March 27, 1986.

sessed with jobs, clubs, and even church activities, that little time remains for family togetherness.

A friend commented to us not long ago that her memories of home were rather negative. Her father taught at a Christian college, and he never had time to be home. Each evening held a committee meeting, a speaking engagement, or some other responsibility.

Christan parents need to learn to live *with*, not *in spite of*, or even *for*, their children (Proverbs 11:29). Family togetherness must be planned; it does not just happen.

PLAY AT HOME

Think about some of the things you can do at home, especially during longer winter evenings. One enriching pastime is reading. When children are small, good books can be read to them. As they get older they may want to read books at their own interest and reading level. The daily newspaper, weekly Sunday school papers, nature stories, or children's classics such as *Heidi, Black Beauty,* or Kipling's stories make for interesting and exciting reading.

Most Christian publishers are now producing series of children's books with biblical teaching such as the Sonflower Series and the Animal Tails Series from Victor Books and *Read Aloud Bible Stories*, by Ella K. Lindvall, and the Children's Bible Basics Series, by Carolyn Nystrom, from Moody Press. These are excellent and can be read to younger children or by older children for their own enjoyment.

Scrapbooks provide a fine family project. Try a picture scrapbook of family outings and events. Or perhaps select a specific subject such as animals, insects, birds, a foreign country, or just the preservation of special school items like poems or stories written by the children. Our daughter had great fun preparing a scrapbook that visualized songs.

Children love to play and perhaps we never outgrow the need for games. Family activities can include table games, puzzles, quizzes, and Ping-Pong.

Hobbies such as collecting coins, stamps, shells, or rocks can be interesting, educational, and will fill many long hours. Some hobbies (painting, woodworking, sewing, or photography) can be carried on all through the adult years.

Our family loved to get out slides and relive vacations or special occasions. The children especially enjoyed hearing funny stories about things they did when they were younger.

We are not ignoring television, perhaps the biggest user of family time. Some television programming has a great deal of good information and entertainment to offer our children. Is television viewing helpful or harmful? One thing is sure, Christian parents dare not ignore their responsibility to control, censor, and guide their children in choosing programs. Many so-called "children's programs" may not be acceptable to Christian parents.

The primary danger of television lies in the likelihood that it will monopolize our time and crowd out many other adventures we could be having with our children. We found that by setting limits on the number of hours of weekly television watching, we provided our children freedom within limits. Each week they could choose programs from our approved list. Very quickly they learned not to use up all of their time too early.

PLAY OUTDOORS

What about the outdoors? The possibilities are unlimited. Depending on your climate, there are sledding, ice skating, tobogganing, touch football, catch, tag, basketball, and other games. The yard can become a ball field, a badminton court, or a place for croquet, lawn darts, or just catching fire-flies after dark.

TAKE SHORT TRIPS

Summer also provides opportunities for picnics at a nearby park, a bicycle ride, or a weekend camping trip. Camping has become quite a popular way of taking a family vacation and can help to bring a family closer together. Setting up the campsite, finding wood, building a fire, and cooking the food all become part of a family project.

Many of these outside activities give Dad wonderful teaching opportunities. Not only will he be able to teach various skills, but also Christian character, attitudes, and good sportsmanship. He might serve as coach or referee for a neighborhood game. Doing such things with our children means a great deal to them, and it models parenting as they will someday practice it.

TRAVEL TOGETHER

Summer usually brings vacation time. As teenagers look back on their childhood, some of their happiest memories are often related to family vacations and holidays.

Vacations should be planned and eagerly anticipated by the entire family. Perhaps we must choose the site on the basis of economics. If we prepare by saving early, family vacations can be enjoyed without sending us into debt for the six months following. A vacation does not have to be long, far away, or expensive to be a happy and positive family experience.

One family decided one year to tour their own city as though they were visitors. They visited all the parks, museums, the zoo, and so on. They enjoyed becoming better acquainted with the city while finding many new and interesting things.

After the location has been decided and you've begun to save the needed money, start gathering interesting things for the children to do in the car. Nobody enjoys several fighting children crammed into a car with two irritated and tired parents. Take along car games, books, and plenty of ideas for passing the hours in a happy sharing time. Keeping a diary, making a scrapbook, taking pictures, and reading travel guides can add pleasure and value to the trip.

REMEMBER SPECIAL OCCASIONS

Birthdays and major holidays should be times when we form happy memories and even family traditions. The experiences need not become ritualistic, but children feel security in the family setting when they know that each Christmas things will happen in somewhat the same pattern. Alma Jones in "Fun with Children" suggests:

> Scientific studies show that maladjustments of children decrease as family recreation increases; also that understanding and confidence between parents and children increase as shared activities and good times increase. (The American Institute of Family Relations, Pub. No. 226)

Does all this sound too idealistic? Is it impossible with our busy schedules? With God's help, it is not only possible, but necessary; our children and their futures are worth the effort.

PRAYING TOGETHER

We talked earlier about praying together as a family. Here we're aiming at husband and wife unified as a single spiritual entity before the Lord. Divorce presents as great a threat to Christians as to society-at-large. We can no longer say that divorce happens only outside our circle.

A greater problem facing the church however, is "practical divorce"—a family situation in which husband and wife live together under the same roof but in a house made empty by the absence of love, interdependence, and warm relationships. The building does not really house a family. It serves as a rest and refueling station for a small group of people who happen to have the same last name.

The happy family cannot claim immunity from problems, but it can handle its problems with understanding and love. Allow us to offer some suggestions to support the spiritual relationship of praying together.

RENEW YOUR VOWS (PSALM 116:14)

Repeatedly review the dynamic of your marriage vows, not necessarily by listening to the tape or watching the video, but by reminding each other verbally of the awesome responsibility you made before God—an eternally binding vow for which every Christian will be held responsible before the judgment seat of Christ.

PRACTICE FORGIVENESS (COLOSSIANS 3:13, 14)

Every quarrel provides an opportunity to practice redemptive attitudes toward each other. The fun of making up is more than just a punch line for jokes about marriage quarrels. Just as parents should be constantly redemptive in every difficult problem situation with children, Mom and Dad should do the same with each other.

FOCUS ON RESPONSIBILITIES, NOT PRIVILEGES (LUKE 12:48)

Both responsibilities and privileges come with every marriage of course, multiplied by roles, duties, good times, bad times, and lots of other experiences we could add. But the person who takes his responsibility seriously keeps a tight rein on relationships and focuses with sensitivity on how he or she can care for and help the other partner.

AVOID STRESSFUL SITUATIONS (MATTHEW 6:25-34)

Try not to get into debt; it just creates arguments over money and budgets. Don't overcommit time, cheating each other and the children. By the way, both of those are important. We did not mean to imply earlier in the chapter that husband and wife should not make time for each other away from the children—that kind of planning carries its own rewards.

RECOGNIZE YOUR VULNERABILITY AND YOUR SPOUSE'S (GALATIANS 6:1-5)

If your needs aren't being met, or if you have reason to think that you are not meeting his or her needs, talk about it. Decide how to work out the problem. Don't be surprised by potential "affairs" or "relationships"—try to spot them way down the road and drive a different direction.

GET HELP WHEN YOU NEED IT (PROVERBS 15:22)

If your pastor or a member of your church staff can help, start there. If the needs stretch beyond that, look for professional help from a Christian counselor. Please remember that a secular counselor or one without established biblical values might very well suggest divorce as a positive alternative to your problems. That's not the kind of advice you need.

ASSUME THAT DIVORCE IS NOT AN OPTION (ROMANS 7:1-3)

We'll talk about that in detail in the next section.

In a frightening but helpful book by Gerald Dahl entitled *Why Christian Marriages Are Breaking Up*, the author summarizes what he has found in working with a number of divorced Christians. It's helpful to take a look at that summary right here:

> Marriages with the "plus" element are characterized by
> • partners who place their relationship above their own personal desires.
> • the willingness of both partners to give each other what they need.
> • the ability of both partners to adjust to changes and growth in the relationship.
> • partners who will work at keeping lines of honest communication open.
> • the willingness of both partners to spend time specifically building and improving the relationship.
> • partners who love Jesus Christ above all else.[3]

---

3. Gerald L. Dahl, *Why Christian Marriages Are Breaking Up* (Nashville: Thomas Nelson, 1979), p. 139.

STAYING TOGETHER

In addition to concentrating on the spiritual unity described above, what kinds of things can a family do to nail down its permanent relationships?

ANTICIPATE PROBLEMS

Above we mentioned one type of problem, the danger of a lustful relationship with someone other than one's spouse. But many other areas trouble families today. In a wide survey conducted by Daniel Yankelovich, parents indicated they wanted help in learning how to talk to each other and their children; in combating rebellion and drug use among their children; in teaching children about religion; in teaching children about sex; and in relating to their children's schooling.[4] This is a wide range of issues, and many more could be added.

Here's the real question: where do *you* need help? What kinds of things should you be reading to keep your family together? How can your church provide classes, literature, encounter groups, or some kind of support system to help keep your family together? Figure it out and then tell the church leaders.

RECOGNIZE THAT INCOMPATIBILITY IS A MYTH

Christian psychiatrist Paul Meier published an article about ten years ago entitled "Divorce Is Never Necessary."[5] In it he argues that the old incompatibility argument is simply an excuse, a cop-out used by couples too proud or too lazy to work out their problems. And the other common excuse, "I just don't love him/her anymore," is a demonstration of unacceptable immaturity. It's a violation of a principle we mentioned earlier in this book—that love does not sustain the marriage but marriage sustains the love.

4. Daniel Yankelovich, et al. *Raising Children in a Changing Society* (N.p.: General Mills, 1977).
5. Paul D. Meier, "Divorce Is Never Necessary," *Action*, Fall 1975.

Meier counsels such people to let behavior recreate the attitude, that is, to attempt the restoration of love by acting in loving ways. Remember how Christ and the church behave like husbands and wives? The Lord tells the Ephesian church in Revelation, "You have forsaken your first love. Remember the height from which you have fallen! Repent and do the things you did at first" (Revelation 2:4-5).

TRUST GOD

Act on faith that God wants you together and will assist you with His sovereign power to the extent that you allow Him to do so. Ultimately the healing of a marriage is the work of God, not of a pastor or a marriage counselor. He may use other people (and often does), but faith in His Word, His power, and His love is the essential ingredient in healing a broken, bleeding marriage.

PREFER ONE ANOTHER

Admit and act upon the mutual obligations of each family member to all the rest. What Paul says about the church in Romans 12:5 can be applied to the family: "Each member belongs to all the others." Recent research downplays the obligation of children to parents and the obligation of parents to children. In the past many families regarded their children as a form of insurance—expecting them to take care of the parents when they became old and sick. Today more than half the parents surveyed by Yankelovich claim that "people have no right to count on their children to help them when they are old or in difficulty."

That same kind of thinking carries over to how these "new breed" parents think about their own children. They feel even more strongly that their children have no obligation to them, regardless of what the parents have done for the children. Particularly younger parents (71 percent of them) and mothers who work full-time (76 percent) take this point of view and in so doing not only violate 1 Timothy 5:4 but create a practical and dangerous independence on the part of the family members. But family members are *not* independent—they are interdependent, and that is very different.

Paul Meier argues that people involved in an unhappy marriage have only three choices. They can elect divorce, thereby opting for the greatest cop-out and the most immature of choices; they can tough it out without working to improve the marriage—a decision not as irresponsible as divorce, but still immature; or they can face up to personal and collective problems and work to build an intimate marriage out of the one they have. According to Meier, that's the only mature choice available. We agree.

Questions for Discussion

1. In what ways does your family have fun together?
2. What kinds of problems arise in connection with planning and taking a vacation? How can some of those problems be avoided?
3. Should a Christian couple ever consider divorce? Support your answer with Scripture.
4. Are you a "new breed" parent? How do your values compare with those of your parents?
5. How valuable are the suggestions offered in the "Praying Together" section? What other ideas would you add?

13

Single Parents—Flying Solo in the Family

At thirty-four, Sally Randolph's life bears no resemblance to what she anticipated fifteen years ago. She has one apartment, one car, two children, one dog—and no husband. She suffers from loneliness, fatigue, disappointment that sometimes borders on depression, and the empty feeling that this frustrating life will continue without improvement for many years to come.

Sally finds little comfort when reading that her minority group is growing rapidly. Nearly half the children born in the mid-seventies will spend time living in one-parent homes before age eighteen. Some estimate that by 1990, more than half the children in all the public schools in America will be living with only one parent, and, in most cases, that parent will be the mother. Thirty-three percent of all divorced fathers never even see their children again.

How can we help Sally? Or, more important, if you are like Sally, what can you do?

COPING WITH LONELINESS

All the research we have done—formal analysis of technical surveys on divorced people and single parents, as well as informal discussions with friends and acquaintances like Sally—indicates that loneliness rises to the top of the pile of problems for single parents. When it occurs with the sudden jolt of an unexpected divorce or death, the shock is intensified. At least three specific areas need to be met to counter loneliness, and, in many cases, the single parent can reach out to find some solutions.

Keep in mind that this book is not aimed at pastors or church boards. If it were, we would couch the counsel of this chapter in terms that would advise the church on how to meet the needs of lonely single parents. We're writing directly to hurting people, and that's why we suggest that initiation may often have to come from the patient and not the doctor. Ephesians 2 stresses the unity of believers in Christ and emphasizes that all members of the family belong in that family to the fullest extent.

> Therefore, remember that formerly you who are Gentiles by birth and called "uncircumcised" by those who call themselves "the circumcision" (that done in the body by the hands of men)—remember that at that time you were separate from Christ, excluded from citizenship in Israel and foreigners to the covenants of the promise, without hope and without God in the world. But now in Christ Jesus you who once were far away have been brought near through the blood of Christ. (Ephesians 2:11-13)

Paul tells us that five kinds of *exclusion* are eliminated through faith in Christ: separation from the Savior, separation from citizenship and the covenant people; separation from the Abrahamic covenant; separation from hope; and separation from knowing God personally. Indeed, one of the blessings of salvation is acceptance—acceptance even of people who have messed up their own lives or have had their lives thrown into turmoil by someone else. Only as lonely people recognize their acceptance by the Heavenly Father can they move on to seek and receive acceptance from others and genuinely claim and practice acceptance of themselves.

THE NEED FOR SELF-WORTH

The next two verses of Ephesians 2, although also highly theological in tone, tell us that God esteems us in Christ.

> For he himself is our peace, who has made the two one and has destroyed the barrier, the dividing wall of hostility, by abolishing in his flesh the law with its commandments and regulations. His purpose was to create in himself one new man out of the two, thus making peace and in this one body to reconcile both of them to God through the cross, by which he put to death their hostility. (Ephesians 2:14-16)

Lonely people who have been through divorce or the death of a spouse tend to suffer from a low level of self esteem. Divorce, at best, demonstrates failure of some kind, however we might place blame or explain reasons. In the midst of all appears the Prince of Peace, who breaks down the walls between warring parties and lays to rest the internal struggles of suffering people. Self-esteem begins, however, with a release from guilt through the act of forgiveness—often elusive self-forgiveness.

THE NEED FOR BELONGING

People are peculiar. Just when the formerly married most desperately need the fellowship of the family of God, they are most tempted to separate from Christian friends who might be judgmental or at least uneasy about their status. How dramatic the words of our passage:

> Consequently, you are no longer foreigners and aliens, but fellow citizens with God's people and members of God's household, built on the foundation of the apostles and prophets, with Christ Jesus himself as the chief cornerstone. (Ephesians 2:19-20)

Loneliness and insecurity surrender their terrors not only to a *sense* of belonging but to the *behavior* of belonging. Happiness follows the wedding of attitude and act. Do people ignore you? Don't let them. If you're excluded from participation and involvement in the ministries of your church, plunge in. If walls of rejection still impede your struggle for acceptance, go to a church where you can feel a sense of belonging and can genuinely be a part of the fellowship.

THE NEED FOR AFFIRMATION

Crucial to coping with loneliness stands the genuine affirmation that singleness is legitimate in the sight of God. We do not write to present views of divorce and remarriage; there are excellent books and articles by competent evangelical theologians on that subject. We want single parents to hear and understand their role in the building of God's temple and to become a part of that spiritual construction (Ephesians 2:21-22). The family may be incomplete at home, but it can be extended and increased through that family of families we call the church.

COPING WITH THE CHILDREN

Broken marriages inflict trauma and a series of crises on more than 1 million children every year. Albert Solnit, director of the Yale Child Study Center in New Haven, Connecticut, claims that "divorce is one of the most serious and complex mental health crisis facing children of the '80s." Child psychologist Lee Salk adds, "The trauma of divorce is second only to death. Children sense a deep loss and feel they are suddenly vulnerable to forces beyond their control."[1]

More than 25,000 children a year are snatched or hidden from one parent by the other, and kidnapped children not found within six months probably won't be found for years.

1. Linda Francke, et al., "The Children of Divorce," *Newsweek*, February 11, 1980, p. 58.

Sally doesn't find this information about children very encouraging. She already feels guilt over the difficulties of handling the children and giving them insufficient time, but she can't seem to find the balance between personal fatigue and the need to spend time with her children. We have no secret formula or final solutions, but here are some suggestions single parents have found helpful.

MINIMIZE STRESS

Many experiences single parents face from day to day create psychological or emotional stress. Much of the pressure can be blamed on *domestic* stress. It invades the homes of single parents because their children struggle to adjust in school and probably have problems with peer relations.

Sometimes domestic stress gets tangled up with *financial stress* because of limited income. The necessity to work full time, often during afternoon and evening hours, makes effective parenting almost impossible. Can this kind of stress be minimized? It helps to simply emphasize the acceptance, self-worth, belonging, and affirmation we talked about earlier. Accept God's forgiveness, and forgive yourself. At least get rid of internal emotional stress.

Second, take the children into your confidence in discussing how to solve family problems. Work out schedules together; utilize the resources of friends or Grandma and Grandpa; let the kids tell you where they hurt and what they need so you can at least pray together about your situation rather than pretend it doesn't exist. Really practice the truth of Matthew 11:28: "Come to me, all you who are weary and burdened, and I will give you rest."

AVOID LATCHKEY PARENTING

Latchkey children are those who come home to empty houses every day after school. If your employer doesn't understand the need for you to be with your children as much as possible, perhaps a change of jobs is important. You may be forced to move to a smaller home or an apartment because of the lesser income, but cramped quarters are better than cramped lives.

PROVIDE ROLE MODELS (PROVERBS 17:6)

Children with missing dads require a Christian male role model; those with missing moms, a female role model. (Boyfriends and girl friends are not the answer here.) If Grandma and Grandpa are still young and active they might serve. Maybe uncles and aunts can help plug the leak. Sunday school teachers, youth group leaders, pastors, or other godly men and women at church all provide a talent pool of examples.

EXPECT IMPROVEMENT

Too many single parents simply anticipate that things will continue to get worse when often there is no justification for such a conclusion. How long does it take a child to adjust to divorce? It varies, of course, with the age of the child, the stability of his life both before and after the divorce, and the way the remaining parent handles the situation.

Generally speaking, we can assume that the situation of all family members involved in a divorce will get worse before it gets better. That's bad news. The good news is that even though the situation seems to be constantly deteriorating, it can improve very suddenly. In one study, psychologists found that five years after their parents' separation, a third of the children seemed to be resilient, an equal number seemed to be muddling through, coping as they could, and the rest were bruised, looking back to life before the divorce with intense longing.[2]

But that research dealt with people who do not have supernatural answers to such problems. The help of Christian friends and family, the support of a godly, loving congregation, and the direct work of God's Holy Spirit in the lives of family members

2. Francke, p. 62.

can dramatically change those statistics in favor of a healthy single parent family.

COPING WITH THE FUTURE

It's not enough that Sally has to face domestic stress and financial stress, she also finds herself constantly in *social stress*. Should she date? Should she think about remarrying? Can she still spend a lot of time with married friends without danger of jealousy or developing improper friendships?

In addition to coping with her own loneliness and the problems of her two children, she has to cope with how to handle her life and their lives over the years and decades ahead. We're pleased to report that Sally's mature outlook has kept her from practicing crisis management in the family. She knows she has to look ahead, and she's doing that by considering certain critical areas of concern.

ACCEPT SINGLENESS

Sally has accepted her singleness and has conquered frustrations about getting remarried. Marriage may come sometime in the future, but she's not going to try to *make* it happen nor will she worry if it doesn't happen. She's determined to be "whole" with or without a husband, and she is asking God to keep her from longing for marriage. Speaking from a secular point of view, Ann Li Puma counsels singles to develop confidence, growth, and progression.

> Equipped with the right balance of these, women will ultimately be able to transform this overwhelming need into something more realistic—more livable. Once that happens, we can all get on with our lives and perhaps even feel fulfilled, with or without a man.[3]

---

3. Ann Li Puma, "Why Are We Afraid to Be Single?" *McCall's*, November 1984, p. 208.

Ms. Li Puma speaks for women, but the principle is the same for men.

TAKE CONTROL

Sally has also determined to take control of finances with confidence rather than fear. Her husband, Jerry, always handled all the finances and now she has everything. But she knows people who can help. Her brother-in-law owns his own business and can quickly teach her how to budget, handle the checking accounts, deal with insurance companies, and plan her financial future. She's bright; she graduated from a community college; and she can read. There's no reason why she can't learn to handle the family's finances as well or perhaps even better than Jerry did over the last ten years.

TRUST GOD

Sally is trusting God to solve the problems of her sexual needs. Her divorce came about quickly, and she has been faced with going from normal sexual relations with her husband to a position of celibacy within a period of less than a year. But she's a committed Christian who understands that God designed sex as a heavenly gift within marriage and that He calls anything else sin. She's determined to utilize the resources of the Word and the control of the Holy Spirit in her life to avoid lust, masturbation, and other problems bound to arise in this area of her life.

CHOOSE SERVICE

Sally has committed herself to becoming a person who *serves*. Yes, to a certain extent, she will have to be served by others. The church will help her; relatives will help; friends will help—and she'll be grateful for all the help she can get. But she wants to be a helping person too. Her first line of ministry, of course, is to her own children, but she expects God to give her opportunity to talk to other single mothers and perhaps even to establish a network of Christian single mothers in her church or community. She plans to discuss that with her pastor and solicit his help.[4]

Sally will make it; many others will not. She'll make it because she understands the problems, knows they can be solved, and knows that the only *real* help comes from the Lord and His people. Recently God has allowed her to meet several strong Christian adults who have been the products of broken homes. She had always assumed that missionaries, pastors, and Christian leaders came out of model families where both parents taught them the things of the Lord all their lives. What an encouragement for her to meet strong Christian people who never knew their own fathers or whose parents abandoned them when they were very young.

Sally has set high goals. By God's grace her children will be loving, committed servants of Jesus Christ, leaders in their churches, godly marriage partners, and biblical parents—even if she has to give her life to that single goal. And that may well be the cost.

Questions for Discussion

1. Have the authors correctly identified the central problems of single parents?
2. How would you describe Sally's life differently? What other solutions or answers are available to her?
3. What other types of stress plague single parents, and how can they be handled?
4. Assess your church's response to single parents. In a spirit of positive, constructive suggestions, how might the congregation improve this phase of its ministry?
5. Review what the authors say about parent-child relations in the single parent home. What would you add?

---

4. For information on how to set up a local Single Parent Christian Fellowship contact Quentin Alfors, The Greater Minneapolis Association of Evangelicals, 6108 Excelsior Blvd., Minneapolis, MN 55416.

Epilogue

Throughout these chapters we have tried to open our hearts and our home to help our readers build better Christian families. We've shared liberally and honestly about our own children and the frustrations and joys we've experienced in parenting.

As our friends all know, we are ordinary people who brought to marriage and parenting the usual mix of problems and potential. A third ingredient made the difference in our lives—a persistence in following what we felt God wanted us to be as partners and parents, coupled with a dependence upon His grace to make that possible. Today our children are young adults in their mid-twenties who love Christ, His church, their parents, and each other.

You can do it too—but not by super-human effort, not by luck, and not by following the ill-founded advice of clamoring secular voices. Success is possible only when you trust the heavenly Father and allow His Spirit to control your family and work out His will in your lives. God bless you!

Selected Bibliography

Adelsperger, Charlotte. *When Your Child Hurts.* Chappaqua, N.Y.: Christian Herald, 1981.

Amstutz, H. Clair. *Growing Up to Love: A Guide to Sex Education for Parents.* Scottsdale, Pa.: Herald Press, 1956.

Anderson, Ray S., and Dennis B. Guernsey. *On Being Family.* Grand Rapids: Eerdmans, 1985.

Bell, Donald A. *The Family in Dialogue.* Grand Rapids: Zondervan, 1968.

Carlson, Lee, ed. *Christian Parenting.* Valley Forge, Pa.: Judson, 1985.

Carter, Elizabeth A., and Monica McGoldrick, eds. *Family Life Circle.* New York: Gardner Press, 1980.

Carter, Velma, and J. Lynn Leavenworth. *Caught in the Middle: Children of Divorce.* Valley Forge, Pa.: Judson, 1985.

Christenson, Larry. *The Christian Family.* Minneapolis: Bethany, 1970.

Christopherson, Victor A. *Child Rearing in Today's Family.* Valley Forge, Pa.: Judson, 1985.

Cole, William Graham. *Sex and Love in the Bible.* New York: Association Press, 1959.

The Concordia Sex Education Series. W. J. Fields, ed., St. Louis: Concordia, 1967.

Curran, Dolores. *Traits of a Healthy Family.* Minneapolis: Winston Press, 1983.

Davidson, Alex. *The Returns of Love.* Downers Grove, Ill.: Inter-Varsity, 1970.

Deen, Edith. *Family Living in the Bible.* New York: Harper & Row, 1963.

DeJong, Alexander. *The Christian Family and Home.* Grand Rapids: Baker, 1959.

Dobson, James. *Dare to Discipline.* Wheaton, Ill.: Tyndale, 1970.

DuVall, Evelyn M. *Why Wait till Marriage?* New York: Association Press, 1965.

Engagement and Marriage. Marriage and Family Research Series. St. Louis: Concordia, 1959.

Fisher-Hunter, W. *The Divorce Problem.* Waynesboro, Pa.: Macneish Publishers, 1952.

Gangel, Kenneth O. *The Family First.* Winona Lake, Ind.: BMH, 1979.

_____. *The Gospel and the Gay.* Nashville: Thomas Nelson, 1978.

Getz, Gene. *The Measure of a Marriage.* Ventura, Calif.: Gospel Light, 1980.

Gow, Kathleen M. *Yes, Virginia, There Is Right and Wrong.* Wheaton, Ill.: Tyndale, 1985.

Grunlan, Stephen. *Marriage and the Family: A Christian Perspective.* Grand Rapids: Zondervan, 1984.

Hazelip, Harold. *Happiness in the Home: Guidelines for Spouses and Parents.* Grand Rapids: Baker, 1985.

Hendricks, Howard, and Jeanne Hendricks, eds. *Husbands and Wives.* Wheaton, Ill.: Victor, forthcoming.

Henrichsen, Walter A. *How to Discipline Your Children.* Wheaton, Ill.: Victor, 1981.

Herron, Orly. *Who Controls Your Child?* Nashville: Thomas Nelson, 1980.

Heth, William A., and Gordon J. Wenham. *Jesus and Divorce.* London: Hodder and Stoughton, 1984.

Kesler, Jay. *The Family Forum.* Wheaton, Ill.: Victor, 1984.

Kesler, Jay, et. al., eds. *Parents and Children.* Wheaton, Ill.: Victor, 1986.

_____. *Parents and Teens.* Wheaton, Ill.: Victor, 1984.

LaHaye, Tim. *The Battle for the Family.* Old Tappan, N.J.: Revell, 1982.

Lewin and Gilmore. *Sex Without Fear.* New York: Medical Research Press, 1950.

Logan, Ben, and Kate Moody, eds. *Television's Awareness Training: The Viewer's Guide for Family and Community.* Nashville: Abingdon, 1980.

MacArthur, John, Jr. *The Family.* Chicago: Moody, 1982.

Miles, Herbert J. *Sexual Happiness in Marriage.* Grand Rapids: Zondervan, 1967.

Money, Royce. *Building Stronger Families.* Wheaton, Ill: Victor, 1984.

Scudder, C. W. *The Family in Christian Perspective.* Nashville: Broadman, 1962.

Sell, Charles M. *Family Ministry.* Grand Rapids: Zondervan, 1981.

Small, Dwight Hervey. *Design for Christian Marriage.* Old Tappan, N.J.: Revell, 1959.

_____. *After You've Said I Do.* Old Tappan, N.J.: Revell, 1968.

Smith, Harold I. *Positively Single.* Wheaton, Ill.: Victor, 1986.

Steele, Paul E. and Charles C. Ryric. *Meant to Last.* Wheaton, Ill.: Victor, 1983.

Stevens, R. Paul. *Married for Good.* Downers Grove, Ill.: InterVarsity, 1986.

Strauss, Richard. *Getting Along with Each Other.* San Bernadino, Calif.: Here's Life, 1985.

_____. *How to Raise Confident Children.* Grand Rapids: Baker, 1984.

Swindoll, Charles R. *Home—Where Life Makes Up Its Mind.* Portland: Multnomah, 1979.

Trobisch, Walter. *I Loved a Girl.* New York: Harper & Row, 1968.

_____. *I Married You.* New York: Harper & Row, 1971.

_____. *Love Is a Feeling to Be Learned.* Downers Grove, Ill.: InterVarsity, 1968.

_____. *My Parents Are Impossible.* Downers Grove, Ill.: InterVarsity, 1971.

_____. *My Wife Made Me a Polygamist.* Downers Grove, Ill.: InterVarsity, 1971.

_____. *Please Help Me, Please Love Me.* Downers Grove, Ill.: InterVarsity, 1970.

Webb, Barbara Owen. *Devotions for Families with Young Readers.* Valley Forge, Pa.: Judson, 1985.

Zuck, Roy B., and Gene A. Getz, eds. *Ventures in Family Living.* Chicago: Moody, 1970.

One Hundred Key Bible Texts on Marriage and Family

Genesis
1:18-30
2:15-25*
3:16†
5:1-3
9:1-7
9:22-27†
12:1-3
19:4-15
19:31-32
24:3-4
30:7, 27-28, 30
38:8-11†
38:12-20

Exodus
12:25-28
20:12
20:14

Leviticus
18:22-30

Numbers
12:1†
27:8-11

Deuteronomy
6:1-9*
8:19
11:18-21
12:12
24:1-4
25:11-12†

Joshua
24:15

Judges
3:5-7
4-5
19:22-23

Ruth
1

1 Samuel
1-4

2 Samuel
12:22-23

Ezra
9:9-12
10:2-3, 14, 17

Psalms
27:10
37:25†
45
68:1-6
94:6
127
128

Proverbs
3:1-2
6:32
10:5
17:2
19:18, 20, 26
22:6
22:15
23:13
29:17
31:10-31*

*Passage of extreme importance
†Passage of difficult interpretation

Song of Solomon
  5:9-16

Isaiah
  28:9-10
  60:17-20

Ezekiel
  16:36-37
  18:1-20*

Malachi
  2:14-16

Matthew
  5:27-32
  18:10
  19:3-10
  22:28

Mark
  5:27-30
  7:21-23

Luke
  2:40-52*
  15:11-32

John
  2:1-11

Acts
  2:46
  10:2
  16:31-34

Romans
  1:26-32
  7:1-3

1 Corinthians
  5:1, 9-11
  6:9-11
  6:14-20
  7:1-7*
  7:8-16†
  7:17-35
  7:36-40
  9:1-6
  13:4-7
  14:34-35

Galatians
  3:26-29

Ephesians
  2:11-22
  3:14
  5:21-33*
  6:1-4*

Colossians
  3:18–4:1*

2 Thessalonians
  3:10-12

1 Timothy
  1:9-10
  2:15†
  3:1-5
  3:11-12
  5:4
  5:8

2 Timothy
  3:1-7
  3:14-15

Titus
  2:4-5

Hebrews
  12:6-14
  13:4

1 Peter
  3:1-7*

Moody Press, a ministry of the Moody Bible Institute, is designed for education, evangelization, and edification. If we may assist you in knowing more about Christ and the Christian life, please write us without obligation: Moody Press, c/o MLM, Chicago, Illinois 60610.